At Issue

Should the
Government Regulate
What People Eat?

Other Books in the At Issue Series:

At Issue

Should the Government Regulate What People Eat?

Ronald D. Lankford, Jr., Book Editor

GREENHAVEN PRESS

A part of Gale, Cengage Learning

Farmington Hills, Mich • San Francisco • New York • Waterville, Maine
Meriden, Conn • Mason, Ohio • Chicago

Elizabeth Des Chenes, *Director, Content Strategy*
Cynthia Sanner, *Publisher*
Douglas Dentino, *Manager, New Product*

LIBRARY OF CONGRESS CATALOGING-IN-PUBLICATION DATA

Should the government regulate what people eat? / Ronald D. Lankford, Jr., book editor.
        pages cm -- (At issue)
    Includes bibliographical references and index.
    ISBN 978-0-7377-6856-5 (hardcover) -- ISBN 978-0-7377-6857-2 (pbk.)
  1. Nutrition policy--United States. I. Lankford, Ronald D., Jr., 1962-
    TX360.U6S564 2014
    363.8'560973--dc23
                                                              2013033393

Printed in the United States of America
1 2 3 4 5 6 7 18 17 16 15 14

Contents

Introduction

In the spring of 2012, New York City's Mayor Bloomberg set off a lively public debate when he suggested banning super-sized sodas. Bloomberg explained the ban:

> Obesity is a nationwide problem, and all over the United States, public health officials are wringing their hands saying, "Oh, this is terrible.". . . New York City is not about wringing your hands; it's about doing something. . . . I think that's what the public wants the mayor to do.[1]

Instead of offering larger sizes, fast-food chains and movie theaters would be restricted to serving cups no larger than sixteen ounces.

While Mayor Bloomberg's tactics proved contentious, his basic premise—that Americans were consuming more fats, sugar, and sodium—went unchallenged. The debate over government regulation, then, was being pushed by a number of factors, including studies on health and obesity, rising health-care costs, and the ineffectiveness of public education in regard to healthy eating.

The direct result of excessive fats and sugar has been weight gain. According to the Centers for Disease Control and Prevention (CDC), one-third of Americans were overweight in 2009–2010. Many studies also suggest that weight gain can be directly connected to health issues. The National Institutes of Health (NIH) addresses obesity in very frank terms:

> Obesity has risen to epidemic levels in the U.S. It causes devastating and costly health problems, reduces life expectancy, and is associated with stigma and discrimination. . . . Thus, the diverse efforts of many federal agencies and public and private organizations will be valuable in working towards reducing obesity.[2]

The National Heart, Lung, and Blood Institute concurred, listing coronary heart disease, high blood pressure, stroke, and Type 2 diabetes as potential risks for those who were overweight.

Even more problematic, many believe, is the growing obesity rates for children. According to the CDC:

- Childhood obesity has more than doubled in children and tripled in adolescents in the past thirty years.

- The percentage of children aged six to eleven years in the United States who were obese increased from 7 percent in 1980 to nearly 18 percent in 2010. Similarly, the percentage of adolescents aged twelve to nineteen years who were obese increased from 5 percent to 18 percent over the same period.

- In 2010, more than one-third of children and adolescents were overweight or obese.[3] The results, as with adults, were increased health problems related to obesity including pre-diabetes, sleep apnea, and bone and joint problems.

In addition to quality of life issues, the health-related problems of obesity also have a financial impact in increased health-care costs. A 2012 Reuters article reported that "obese men rack up an additional $1,152 a year in medical spending. . . ."[4] The average health-care cost for obese women was $3,271 compared with $512 for the nonobese. These costs equaled "$190 billion a year in additional medical spending as a result of obesity. . . ."[5]

In the United States, these costs impact all Americans, obese or not in the higher cost of health care. These health-care costs include private and group policies as well as the cost of government programs such as Medicare and Medicaid. Emilie Openchowski notes in *American Progress*:

Obesity-related health care costs are partly paid for by non-obese Americans through taxes to support Medicare and Medicaid and higher overall insurance premiums. In much the same way that nonsmokers end up paying in part for health care costs associated with smoking tobacco, or the insured pay for emergency care for the uninsured, everyone shoulders the burden for needed health services. This means we all can expect taxes and premiums to soar if the number of obese people grows as projected.[6]

The underlying problem is that health-care costs and taxes will need to continually increase to match growing obesity rates. In one study, it was projected that, "42 percent of Americans will be obese by 2030, and 11 percent of the population will be severely obese."[7]

A third issue when considering whether what people eat should be regulated is the perceived ineffectiveness of past government efforts. Specifically, the ineffectiveness of government educational efforts related to healthy eating and the health dangers of obesity. As Neil Munro notes in the *Daily Caller*, "The decades-long federal campaign against obesity has achieved a perfect record of failure."[8] Munro writes:

Since 2000, federal medical-professionals and their allies in the anti-obesity sector have pleaded, cajoled, nagged, stigmatized, lobbied, taxed, litigated and regulated, but the nation's collective belt size has steadily notched upwards, according to the CDC's data.[9]

In 2007, *USA Today* reported that the United States federal government spent $1 billion on nutrition education. Overwhelmingly, however, the programs funded by this money failed to have an impact.

With growing obesity rates, higher health-care costs, and ineffective educational programs, many people—in schools, in state and federal government, and at home—are looking for new solutions. One of these solutions is for the government to regulate what people eat, limiting fats, sugars, and sodium. As with Mayor Bloomberg's attempt to regulate soda size, however, the government regulation of food and beverages remains very controversial.

Even while many commentators, legislators, and school officials agree on the problem (increasing obesity leads to greater health-care costs), there is no consensus on a solution. Many argue that these issues are the responsibility of individuals and families, not the government. Others argue that government intervention is a necessity, especially to protect children. Still others, including the fast food and soft drink companies, argue that healthy choices are already available to consumers who are willing to make those choices. Despite a lack of consensus, the growing awareness of obesity and health-related problems promises to keep the issue of the government regulation of food in news headlines.

The contributors to *At Issue: Should the Government Regulate What People Eat?* examine this issue from a variety of perspectives, including the effectiveness of past regulations, the politics of weight loss, and attempts to change school lunch programs.

Notes

1. As quoted in Michael M. Grynbaum, "New York Plans to Ban Sale of Big Sizes of Sugary Drinks," *New York Times*, May 30, 2012. http://www.nytimes.com/2012/05/31/nyregion /bloomberg-plans-a-ban-on-large-sugared-drinks.html?page wanted=all&_r=0.
2. "About NIH Obesity Research," NIH, accessed July 2013. http://obesityresearch.nih.gov/about/about.aspx.
3. "Childhood Obesity Facts," CDC, accessed July 2013. http:// www.cdc.gov/healthyyouth/obesity/facts.htm.
4. Sharon Begley, "As America's Waistline Expands, Costs Soar," Reuters, April 30, 2012. http://www.reuters.com/article/2012 /04/30/us-obesity-idUSBRE83T0C820120430.
5. *Ibid.*

6. Emilie Openchowski, "Linking Obesity and Health Care," Center for American Progress, May 21, 2012. http://www.americanprogress.org/issues/healthcare/news/2012/05/21/11514/linking-obesity-and-health-care.

7. *Ibid.*

8. Neil Munro, "Anti-Obesity Programs Fail, So Feds Try Again," *Daily Caller*, July 20, 2011. http://dailycaller.com/2011/07/20/anti-obesity-programs-fail-so-feds-try-again.

9. *Ibid.*

1

Government Should Regulate Corporations That Sell Unhealthy Food

Raj Patel

Raj Patel is a British-born American journalist, and author of Stuffed and Starved *(2008).*

Recently, the authors of an article in Nature *suggested that sugar should be regulated. Like tobacco or alcohol, sugar—in large quantities—is unhealthy. While the food industry has argued that it also manufactures healthy snacks, snacking itself has added to the American waistline. While food manufacturers will fight all change, the* Nature *article invites Americans to imagine a world in which food is no longer controlled by a powerful industry.*

In the fall of 2008, San Francisco polished its progressive credentials by banning something. From October 1, 2008, the sale of cigarettes was prohibited in certain places. You could still buy them in convenience stores, of course, and bodegas, gas stations, and even the occasional bar. But the city thought that perhaps it was a bad idea to allow them to be sold in pharmacies. As the city attorney, Dennis Herrera, put it: "Consumers—and especially young people—should reasonably expect pharmacies to serve their health needs, not to enable our leading cause of preventable death."

Pharmacy and tobacco executives were apoplectic. The Walgreens pharmacy chain argued that they needed to be allowed to sell cigarettes so that they might counsel people on how to quit. The tobacco industry was upset too. From the hallowed garden of constitutional law, it argued that the ban was an infringement of its First Amendment rights to free speech. Big Smoke argued that it was being muzzled by an over-reaching government marching down the road to tyranny. The judge who heard the case took a dim view of this logic, pointing out that while advertising is a form of free speech, "selling cigarettes isn't." The ban continues.

The cigarette industry survives, as does its advertising. Cigarette companies' rights to free speech have, however, been curtailed on grounds of public health, and for the health of children above all. Joe Camel isn't familiar to children today, as he was in the 1970s, because most people agree that it's probably a bad idea to have a hip smoking cartoon character to which kids aspire, even if the company behind it swears blind it was just going after the pro-dromedary slice of the adult market.

Alcohol is similarly circumscribed, again with an eye to public health and, again, with a particular concern for young people. But if public health is a legitimate reason to curb corporations' advertising to kids, why limit bans to cigarettes and booze, and not include, say, unhealthy food?

Why allow an industry that profits from the sale of unhealthy food at all?

Regulating Sugar

A paper in the latest [February 2012] issue of *Nature* by Robert Lustig, Laura Schmidt, and Claire Brindis fuels the debate, pointing to the long-term similarities of sugar and alcohol consumption.

The paper's authors freely admit that a little sugar is fine, but "a lot kills—slowly." They argue that sugar meets the same four generally accepted public health criteria used to regulate alcohol: it is unavoidable, toxic, has the potential for abuse, and has a negative impact on society. Which is why they suggest restrictions on advertising of sugary processed foods, lauding another of San Francisco's bans—the one that prevents toys being given away with unhealthy fast food meals.

Given the food industry's power, and fears of a nanny state, it's unsurprising that the paper's authors are caught in a flame war.

I side with the American Psychological Association in thinking that advertising to children is unconscionable. Rather than dwell on the First Amendment issue, which strikes me as an easy case to make, I think it's worth addressing a deeper question underlying the San Francisco cigarette-in-pharmacy ban: Why allow an industry that profits from the sale of unhealthy food at all?

Returning to tobacco is helpful. Stanford historian Robert Proctor's life work has been to expose the lies of the tobacco industry. In his magisterial new book, *Golden Holocaust*, he makes the case for the abolition of the industry entirely. . . . Cigarettes, when used according to manufacturer instructions, will lead to death. So why harbor tobacco's peddlers? (This argument, incidentally, won't come as a surprise to R.J. Reynolds, who subpoenaed the manuscript because Proctor had in the past testified as an expert witness against the industry.)

The history of banning things is admittedly inglorious. The war on drugs, Prohibition, and censorship have few fans. There are two reasons why Proctor's proposals are different. First, most smokers don't want to be smokers. "Only about three percent of people who drink are alcoholic," he says. "If smokers could choose freely, then they would choose not to smoke. Nicotine is not a recreational drug. . . . It's really fundamentally different."

Second, he doesn't want to ban smoking. The language of abolition—not prohibition—is well chosen. Proctor doesn't yearn for the criminalization of smokers, nor does he foresee the end of cigarettes or tobacco. He's simply arguing that the industry that profits from it oughtn't to exist in a society that has a minimum concern with public health. If you want to smoke, you're free to grow and cure your own tobacco, he suggests.

Big Food's Defense

The analogy of tobacco with food isn't perfect, clearly. People who eat Twinkies often want to eat Twinkies, and we all need to eat. But it's increasingly common to see the medical literature push forward an understanding of sugar addiction and it's also true that our food choices are far from free, in no small part because of the commercial and cultural power of the food industry. Weaned as most of us are on Big Food's free speech, we ought to be suspicious of our instincts when it comes to food.

The food industry is an oligopoly that has transformed not only what we eat but how we eat, and what we think of food.

This week's *Nature* article doesn't argue for the abolition of Big Food, but indicts the industry nonetheless: "Sugar is cheap, sugar tastes good, and sugar sells, so companies have little incentive to change." Limiting the power of these corporations to sell their products—just as we limit alcohol and tobacco companies—ought to be widely agreed, and the battle among health professionals in the years to come will see the transformation of this proposition into an axiom.

The food industry tastes its own blood in the water, and is responding aggressively to the nicks and cuts from public health professionals. It's unwise to underestimate the chutzpah of an industry that spread trans fats across the Western diet in the 20th century, and made a marketing pitch of their removal in the 21st. So the industry has adopted a strategy that counters a pound of sugar with an ounce of nutrition.

Derek Yach, senior vice president of Global Health and Agriculture Policy at PepsiCo, offers Sun Chips as a food that "would do very well on almost every nutrition criteria." The problem is that while they're moderately better than other chips, they're still chips, and part of a business whose main profit derives from food high in salt, fat, and sugar. More important, Sun Chips are still a snack food—the growth of which, some argue, is the main engine for expanding American waistlines.

A World Without Big Food

The breadth of products controlled by the food industry— amply toxic and less so—is itself a symptom of a deeper problem that has public health symptoms, but a political economic cause. The food industry is an oligopoly that has transformed not only what we eat but how we eat it, and what we think of food. Which is why the logic of Proctor's argument as it could apply to the food industry waits in the wings—for now. It's hard to entertain the abolition of the food industry, because it's difficult to imagine ourselves in a world without PepsiCo, Nestlé, Kraft (formerly part of Philip Morris), and friends, and their product lines.

Few have lived in a world in which a handful of corporations don't run the food system. The food industry has made our world theirs. Instant meals and ready calories are as much a part of the fabric of late capitalist life as the culture in which they're acceptable. Excising corporations from an economy that has come to depend on their products addresses the problem of added toxins in food. But it does little to change the circumstance that renders those foods a caloric raft for the poor, nor does it address deeper injustices within the food system spawned by corporate power.

But a better food system needn't be limited to one where food giants behave a little better because they are taxed and hushed a little. Lustig and colleagues argue for limits to corporate power in food because, by adding sugar to almost everything they make, they make us less free as consumers. Extending Proctor's argument to those very corporate powers invites us to imagine what a world without Big Food might look like—and dream ourselves freer still.

2

Government Regulations Should Promote Healthier Eating Choices

Laura A. Schmidt

Laura A. Schmidt is a professor of health policy in the school of medicine at the University of California at San Francisco.

While sugar in the American diet has created health problems, heavy regulation has the potential to create new problems. In the past, the government relied on health education, but this too proved ineffectual. The problem is that Americans tend to eat whatever is in front of them, which, thanks to the food industry, is often filled with sugar. Instead of banning sugar or other substances, the government needs to offer incentives to provide more choices for the consumer. If the healthy product is as easy to find on the supermarket shelf and purchase as the sugar-filled product, Americans will make better choices.

The overabundance of sugar in the American diet isn't just making us fat. It's hurting our health. We were all raised to think of sugar as benign "empty calories." But science shows that too much sugar—i.e., the amount consumed by the average American—leads to high blood pressure, dyslipidemia, fatty liver, insulin resistance and pancreatitis. Excessive sugar consumption leads to metabolic disease, which leads to the main chronic illnesses that will eventually kill most of us:

heart disease, stroke, cancer, as well as diabetes. Sugar overload also creates a cascade of chemical changes in the body, turning off the hormones that tell us when we've eaten enough, and affecting brain neurotransmitters that leave us craving more sugar.

The point is that too much sugar has all of these harmful effects on health *in addition to* its role in America's obesity epidemic. This growing awareness has led to a trenchant public debate about whether it isn't time to regulate sugar.

The debate about regulating sugar is, however, based on a false assumption: If we regulate the stuff, we will wind up with government bureaucrats telling us what we can and can't eat. Fortunately, there are alternatives that lie somewhere between political extremes—in gentle, market-based alterations that improve health while actually *increasing* choice.

Failed Health Education

For decades, America's main strategy to prevent obesity and metabolic disease has been education: nutrition labels, public service announcements, and mainly, school-based health education. There is now solid evidence that health education doesn't work to change behavior, especially for substances with abuse potential. It can change attitudes and knowledge, but it doesn't have lasting effects on what people actually do.

Most of the time, most of us tend to eat and drink what's in front of us.

Most of us intuitively understand why health education doesn't work. We may try for a while to eat healthy by limiting added sugar. But we quickly find that it actually takes a lot of planning, money, and effort to *not* eat sugar, and that many of us crave the stuff due to effects on the brain's "reward center."

The fundamental problem is that we live in what addiction researchers call *a saturated environment.* You know you live in a sugar-saturated environment when you have to go out of your way to find a drinking fountain or a fresh apple. But junk food counters and vending machines line the walls of workplaces, airports, shopping centers and even schools. Our saturated environment doesn't just make sugar-laden products easy to get. *It makes them hard to avoid.*

At a minimum, there should be a level playing field for consumers to choose.

In their *New York Times* bestseller, *Nudge,* two professors from the University of Chicago School of Economics (a bastion of conservative politics) point out what public health researchers have known for years: Most of the time, most of us tend to eat and drink what's in front of us. *The best way to promote healthy weight and metabolism is to make the healthy stuff cheaper and easier to get than the unhealthy stuff.* These authors describe a simple experiment that vividly illustrates the point. A school cafeteria lady put the low-fat milk on the front shelf while the sugary drinks went up high and in back. Guess what? The lunch lady increased milk consumption while helping kids get off the sweet stuff throughout the school.

The "Nudge"

Effective public health regulation is all about the nudge. It's about making healthier options easier and cheaper to get, and asking people to reach a little farther for products harmful to health. More importantly, it's about nudging producers and distributors to increase the availability of healthier alternatives through market incentives: by ending subsidies and pro-rating taxes based on how much sugar has been added to the product. There is now a vast body of international research showing that such simple strategies are easy to implement and tangibly affect population health.

But one question remains: How is it possible that regulating sugar will actually *increase* personal choice? Well, we all know that junk food companies have massive marketing departments working 24/7 to figure out ways to nudge us towards their products. That's why candy in the supermarket checkout aisle is at eye level for a child, and why the milk is at the back end of the store. That's why 80% of the foods in America are laced with added sugar—to make us want to buy more and more of these products. *What we need is a nudge back*. At a minimum, there should be a level playing field for consumers to choose.

There is one assumption that lies at the heart of these new public health regulatory solutions—that, at the end of the day, most Americans want to live long, healthy lives and would prefer a smorgasbord of options for what they choose to drink and eat. We don't want anybody—government or corporations—telling us we can or can't have a soda. But we do want choosing health to be an easy option, if not the default. This assumption, unlike others framing the current sugar debate, seems like a reasonable one to make.

Of course nobody wants a government bureaucrat telling us what we can eat and drink. But neither should we want to live in an environment where powerful corporations tell us what to eat and drink, by continuously nudging us toward products that undermine our chances for a long, healthy life.

3

Government Food Nannies Eat Away at Our Freedom and Prosperity

Carrie Lukas

Carrie Lukas is the managing director for the politically conservative Independent Women's Forum.

As cities like New York threaten to regulate what Americans eat and drink, the public should be warned. Regulating the American diet does not work. Even government officials seem to be aware that most regulations are little more than empty gestures. Unfortunately, regulations also have the unwanted side-effect of hurting businesses.

Mayor Michael Bloomberg's push to ban the sale of large, sugary drinks in New York City made headlines last week, but it's really just another dog-bites-man political story. For years, government officials from Washington D.C. down to local school districts have been busily writing regulations and levying new taxes in an attempt to control what Americans eat.

The public be warned: History shows that Americans aren't likely to lose weight as a result of such efforts. We will, however, shed real freedom and be left with a trimmed-down economy.

Bloomberg himself let slip why the measure is unlikely to meaningfully change New Yorkers' calorie consumption. In beating back a question suggesting the ban would inappropriately limit consumer choice, he scoffed, "Your argument, I guess, could be that it's a little less convenient to have to carry two 16-ounce drinks to your seat in the movie theater rather than one 32 ounce."

The Mayor is right. Those seeking a big gulp of soda will be able to get one. This new rule wouldn't limit costumers to just one drink purchase or forbid free refills. That means customers who want more will have to pay extra for two cups or make another trip to the soda dispenser. A good follow up question to the Mayor would have been, what's the point, then, of imposing the ban at all?

Even so-called "sin taxes" on soda and sugar are a poor method of discouraging obesity.

Bloomberg explained that rather than just hand-wringing about stubbornly high rates of obesity, citizens expect their leaders to "do something." The Mayor seems to assume New Yorkers won't mind that that "something" is little more than an empty gesture.

The truth is most of governments' efforts to cajole Americans to eat healthier have had little success. Policymakers have forced restaurants to display calorie information on the assumption that informed customers would opt for lower-calorie items. Yet research suggests that most patrons ignore the information, and those who actually bother to review calorie counts don't make healthier decisions as a result.

Washington also has expanded school-based feeding programs, in part to help fight obesity by giving kids healthier food. Analysts have now learned that many kids effectively have two breakfasts, one at school and one at home, as a result, ironically adding to their weight problems. Even so-called "sin taxes" on soda and sugar are a poor method of discouraging obesity. Studies show that soda taxes miss their target since obese people tend to already opt for diet sodas, and unsurprisingly, some states with these tax regimes also have the largest obesity problems.

Americans are used to government regulations and tax schemes failing to work as intended. If all this food regulation were just a waste of time, Americans might shrug it off. Yet this government meddling sucks resources from our undernourished economy, aggravating our nation's truly pressing national ailment: joblessness.

How is it that America . . . is now a nation of food police dictating how large a Coke you can buy?

Mayor Bloomberg argues that businesses hit with the ban won't suffer because they can charge consumers more for smaller drinks and find other ways to make up for lost sales. Maybe. But the changes they make will also affect their suppliers who, if the ban works at all, will move less product and have to reduce workers and production. Businesses will also lose time and money making sense of the regulations. Coffee houses will have to take care to follow the new guidelines to see if their baristas' latest concoctions safely fall under the "latte" genre, and therefore can be sold in unlimited quantities, or if they're plain old sweetened coffee, thus making them illegal in containers larger than 16 ounces.

This is just another of the reams of regulations that are a growing burden on business, especially small businesses. When testifying before Congress, Andy Puzder, CEO of CKE Restaurants (which operates the Hardees and Carl's Jr. restaurant chains), explained how such regulations affect franchises and small food industry businesses. He warned that the menu labeling requirements in ObamaCare alone would cost his company $1.5 million, about a fifth of what it invested in starting up new restaurants in 2010. Outlawing large sodas and juice drinks may seem relatively minor, but even a small change in income can have a significant impact on small stores and restaurants with slim margins, and end up discouraging job creation (job loss may also result) at some city establishments.

Of course, Mr. Bloomberg's regulations are sure to create a few new jobs: New York City will be seeking bureaucrats to ensure no one sneaks regular soda into those illegally large diet soda containers.

That too creates real costs, the greatest of which is dignity. How is it that America, land of the free and home of the brave, is now a nation of food police dictating how large a Coke you can buy?

4

New York City's Ban on Soda Size Is Imperfect but Needed

Jonny Bowden

Jonny Bowden is an expert on weight loss and nutrition and author of The 150 Healthiest Foods on Earth.

Government regulation often is unhelpful, and it frequently limits personal liberty. But many people do not mind regulation when it limits something considered bad or harmful. Sugar has fueled a health crisis in America, and it is time to get serious about regulating it. While a particular regulation—like the New York City plan to regulate soda size—may be imperfect, it is nonetheless a start in the right direction.

On Tuesday, March 12 [2012], on the day before it was scheduled to go into effect, a state judge struck down New York City Mayor Michael Bloomberg's proposed ban on jumbo-sized sodas, triggering a paroxysm of editorials about the nanny state and the future of civilization.

OK, everybody, let's take a deep breath.

I hate the nanny state as much as you do, but that dislike comes with an asterisk.

See, it's not the idea of regulation *per se*, that I dislike. It's the fact that the government is a bumbling mess, gets few things right and tends to eventually screw up the few things they do get right—like Medicare and the VA [Veterans Administration]. So the last thing I want is a bunch of government bureaucrats telling me what I can eat, who I can sleep with, what I can smoke, who I can marry, what my female friends can do with their bodies, or any of a dozen other things they have no business telling me to do (or *not* do).

But I—like many fellow nanny-state-haters on both sides of the aisle—sing a very different tune about government when a Hurricane Katrina appears or a bumbling terrorist tries to light his underwear on fire on a 747. We're perfectly happy that there are rules and regulations that prevent our neighbors from erecting a 10-foot monument to the KKK on the town square, or a local factory from pumping mercury into the air, or a strip club from opening next door to St. John's Cathedral. We *want* government oversight and regulation when it protects us from what we want to be protected from. When it "protects" us from what we don't want to be protected from, we'd prefer it to leave us the heck alone, thank you very much.

And we like government least of all when it interferes with our personal liberty.

Which brings us to the heart of the soda problem.

Poisoned by Sugar

Look, I get the whole "personal liberty" argument. Really, I do. I listen to Adam Carolla and Dennis Prager. I love Jon Stewart. There are times when, if I squint, even Ron Paul seems to make sense for a minute, particularly when he gets started on the idiocy of the government preventing me from consuming raw milk. I even understand the sentiment behind the slippery-slope argument (today our soda, tomorrow our guns!). Believe me, I get it.

So in a perfect world, we'd have as little government interference as possible.

But this is very far from that perfect world. And in the world we actually live in, we're being poisoned by sugar.

Despite the massive protests and multi-milliondollar campaigns by the sugar industry, the Corn Refiners Association and others to convince us that sugar is a perfectly harmless substance that can be incorporated "in moderation" in a healthy diet, the truth is very different. Sugar is an addictive substance that we consume to the tune of 150 pounds per capita per year, and it's destroying our health and destroying our children.

And we have two basic choices. We can fail to act, citing the sanctity of personal freedom and the encroachment of the dreaded nanny-state. . . or we can do something.

This isn't the place to go over the massive evidence that sugar is the culprit in the American diet. For those who didn't get the memo, I recommend the terrific new book, *Salt Sugar Fat: How the Food Giants Hooked Us*, Dr. Robert Lustig's brilliant *Fat Chance: Beating the Odds Against Sugar, Processed Food, Obesity and Disease* (or his lecture, "Sugar: The Bitter Truth" on YouTube), or—if you just want to get your feet wet—Mark Bittman's wonderfully clear and pithy "Regulating Our Sugar Habit" in the *New York Times* a few weeks ago. Even a superficial look at the literature will convince all but the most entrenched supporters of Big Food that sugar—and its nearly identical twin, high-fructose corn syrup—are not innocent bystanders in the skyrocketing rates of obesity, diabetes and heart disease. We're not fat, sick, tired and depressed because they took phys-ed out of the school system or because everyone watches too much television. Sure, those things matter, but they pale in comparison to the effect of mainlining a deadly white substance that literally creates hormonal havoc and appetite dysregulation, all the while promoting metabolic syndrome, diabetes, obesity and heart disease.

What to do, what to do?

Protecting Children from Sugar

Well, desperate times call for desperate measures, and when it comes to sugar, these are desperate times indeed.

The defenders of personal freedom who are applauding the strikedown of the Bloomberg initiative would be appalled at the suggestion that heroin dealers be allowed to peddle their wares in schoolyards. Yet these same folks bristle at the mere suggestion of regulations which would make it even marginally more difficult for sugar pushers to do the same thing. These champions of "personal liberty" tell us that regulations don't take the place of parenting—that keeping kids out of McDonald's should be the job of parents, not the government. (I often wonder if the people making this argument actually have kids, and if they do, I wonder if they live in the real world. But I digress.) None of these good folks would ever agree to having crack cocaine sold in their kids' school cafeteria because to ban it would be an affront to personal liberty, and because "it should be the goal of good parenting" to keep kids from buying this stuff in the first place.

We're up against a serious enemy here folks, and its name is sugar.

Look, back in the late '90s I worked for Coca-Cola for a year, during the time they introduced Dasani water. I sat on the advisory board for Dasani, wrote articles about the benefits of purified water, and worked closely with a lot of execs from Coke. They were nice people. Really. But as a corporation, they're selling death. Seriously. And they're selling it to children, and they've sold it to us, and there's no getting around the fact that the stuff they—and other soda manufacturers are selling—is a wildly destructive substance with no redeeming qualities that is destroying the health of America and any other nation in which they can get a foothold.

A Good Place to Start

Are the soda makers the only culprits? Hell, no. (And they'll be the first to tell you so!) But they're a damn good place to start.

Did the Bloomberg proposal have faults? You bet. Did it have loopholes? Sure. Would it present an enforcement nightmare? Probably, although not nearly as bad as critics have suggested.

But that does that mean we sit back and do nothing?

No. We're up against a serious enemy here folks, and its name is sugar. In all its forms, including the kind that's marketed as healthy (agave nectar syrup, anyone?). Including the stuff that turns into sugar in a heartbeat, also marketed as healthy. (Breakfast candy? I mean, cereal?)

Because there is no perfect intervention, does that mean we don't intervene at all?

Sure, making it illegal to sell obscenely sized vats of sugar and chemicals is a logistical nightmare, fraught with problems and far from ideal.

But it's a start.

I have huge qualms about giving our government more power than it already has over what we can put into our bodies—particularly when that government has demonstrated jaw-dropping stupidity when it comes to nutrition in general. But whenever I think that the "solution" is worse than the problem, I remember how bad sugar really is and what it's doing to our health, our well-being and ultimately, even our national security.

And then I remember something that's served me well to remember in a lot of endeavors, something that is a great antidote to my—and others'—natural tendency toward inaction in the face of what seems like an insurmountable problem:

"The greatest enemy of a good plan is the search for a perfect one."

Is the Bloomberg initiative a perfect plan? Far from it.

But right now it's all we've got, and it's better than nothing. And man, we better start somewhere.

Why not here?

5

New York City's Ban on Soda Size Will Be Ineffective

Jacob Sullum

Jacob Sullum is a senior editor at Reason *magazine and Reason-
.com and a nationally syndicated columnist.*

*New York City's plan to limit the size of sodas to sixteen ounces
has one flaw: It will not work. The plan assumes that soda is
causing Americans to gain weight with little proof. Furthermore,
many beverages—such as high-calorie fruit juices—are exempted
from the ban. The bigger problem, however, is that any govern-
mental ban would limit personal freedom.*

Defending his proposal to fight obesity by restricting soft
drink sizes, New York Mayor Michael Bloomberg says, "I
think that's what the public wants the mayor to do." If the
public wanted it, of course, there would be no need for the
government to require it. Bloomberg's plan makes sense only
to the extent that it changes consumers' decisions by limiting
their options—specifically, by decreeing that restaurants, food
carts, movie theaters, and concession stands at sports arenas
may not sell more than 16 ounces of most sugar-sweetened
beverages in one cup or bottle. Yet *The New York Times* reports that Bloomberg cast doubt on the rationale for this rule
right out of the gate:

> The mayor, who said he occasionally drank a diet soda "on a
> hot day," contested the idea that the plan would limit
> consumers' choices, saying the option to buy more soda
> would always be available.

"Your argument, I guess, could be that it's a little less convenient to have to carry two 16-ounce drinks to your seat in
the movie theater rather than one 32 ounce," Mr. Bloomberg
said in a sarcastic tone. "I don't think you can make the case
that we're taking things away."

If so, what's the point? If the added inconvenience of car-
rying two containers does not deter people from drinking as
much soda as they otherwise would, how can Bloomberg pos-
sibly claim his restrictions will make people thinner?

Are Sodas the Problem?

The answer is that Bloomberg and his health commissioner,
Thomas Farley, say whatever pops into their heads, without
regard to logic or evidence. Consider:

In New York City, where more than half of adults are obese
or overweight, Dr. Thomas Farley, the health commissioner,
blames sweetened drinks for up to half of the increase in
city obesity rates over the last 30 years. About a third of
New Yorkers drink one or more sugary drinks a day, according to the city. Dr. Farley said the city had seen higher obesity rates in neighborhoods where soda consumption was
more common.

Correlation = causation. QED. If that is the quality of
Farley's science, perhaps we should not ask how he came up
with the estimate that sweetened drinks account for "up to
half" of the increase in obesity rates since the early 1980s.
That statement, after all, is consistent with the possibility that
sweetened drinks account for none of the increase.

Even if we accept Farley's claims about soda's role in rising
obesity rates, it does not follow that Bloomberg's plan will
have a measurable impact on New Yorkers' waistlines. There
are reasons to doubt that it will, starting with the mayor's ob-
servation that extra-thirsty customers can always buy another
16-ounce drink (which might actually result in the consump-

tion of more calories, assuming their usual serving is between 16 and 32 ounces). Nor will undercover health inspectors monitor the city's fast food restaurants to prevent diners from availing themselves of free refills; the regulations graciously let them drink as much soda as they want, as long as they do it 16 ounces at a time. The size rule does not apply at all to convenience stores, supermarkets, or vending machines, so Big Gulps, giant Slurpees, and large bottles of soda will still be readily available. Bloomberg also plans to exempt fruit juices, which typically have more calories per ounce than sugar-sweetened soda, and milk-based drinks. So while New Yorkers won't be allowed to order 20 ounces of Coke (240 calories), they will still be able to get a 20-ounce Starbucks whole-milk latte (290 calories) or even a 24-ounce Double Chocolaty Frappuccino (520 calories), not to mention a 20-ounce milkshake (about 800 calories).

Limiting Personal Choice

In other words, Bloomberg is right when he says there will still be lots of opportunities for New Yorkers to consume large quantities of high-calorie drinks, which means he does not even have a sound paternalistic justification for his meddling. He is screwing with people not to protect them from their own foolish choices but just to create the appearance of doing so. Or maybe just because he can.

The *Times* notes that Bloomberg "has made public health one of the top priorities of his lengthy tenure" with "a series of aggressive regulations," including "bans on smoking in restaurants and parks" and "a prohibition against artificial trans fat in restaurant food." It adds that "the measures have led to occasional derision of the mayor as Nanny Bloomberg, by those who view the restrictions as infringements on personal freedom." Is there any other reasonable way to view such restrictions? It is one thing to argue (as Bloomberg presumably would) that the restrictions are justified by the government's supposed duty to minimize morbidity and mortality by preventing people from taking risks (its "highest duty," according to Bloomberg). But it is patently absurd for Bloomberg to claim he is not limiting freedom when he uses force to stop people from doing something that violates no one's rights, whether it's selling donuts fried in trans fat, lighting up in a bar whose owner has chosen to allow smoking on his own property, or ordering a 20-ounce soda in a deli. When, as in this case, his arrogant, healthier-than-thou interference has, by his own admission, zero chance of achieving its stated goal, that fact hardly makes his arbitrary use of government power less objectionable.

6

Regulations Do Change Eating Behavior

Marion Nestle

Marion Nestle is the Paulette Goddard Professor in the Department of Nutrition, Food Studies, and Public Health at New York University. She is author of Why Calories Count: From Science to Politics, *as well as* Food Politics *and* What to Eat. *She also blogs at foodpolitics.com.*

Despite complaints about the government regulation of food, one fact remains: it works. Since attempts to limit advertising have been protected as free speech, city governments have searched for new methods of creating healthier eating options for consumers. Banning items, research shows, allows easier access to healthy choices. In time, perhaps, even the federal government will adapt similar regulations.

M y monthly, first Sunday column in the *San Francisco Chronicle*:

Q: *I still don't get it. Why would a city government think that a food regulation would promote health when any one of them is so easy to evade?*

A: Quick answer: because they work.

As I explained in my July discussion of Richmond's proposed soda tax, regulations make it easier for people to eat healthfully without having to think about it. They make the default choice the healthy choice. Most people choose the default, no matter what it is.

Telling people cigarettes cause cancer hardly ever got anyone to stop. But regulations did. Taxing cigarettes, banning advertising, setting age limits for purchases, and restricting smoking in airplanes, workplaces, bars and restaurants made it easier for smokers to stop.

Economists say, obesity and its consequences cost our society $190 billion annually in health care and lost productivity, so health officials increasingly want to find equally effective strategies to discourage people from over-consuming sugary drinks and fast food.

Research backs up regulatory approaches. We know what makes us overeat: billions of dollars in advertising messages, food sold everywhere—in gas stations, vending machines, libraries and stores that sell clothing, books, office supplies, cosmetics and drugs—and huge portions of food at bargain prices.

Research also shows what sells food to kids: cartoons, celebrities, commercials on their favorite television programs, and toys in Happy Meals. This kind of marketing induces kids to want the products, pester their parents for them, and throw tantrums if parents say no. Marketing makes kids think they are supposed to eat advertised foods, and so undermines parental authority.

Public health officials look for ways to intervene, given their particular legislated mandates and authority. But much as they might like to, they can't do much about marketing to children. Food and beverage companies invoke the First Amendment to protect their "right" to market junk foods to kids. They lobby Congress on this issue so effectively that they even managed to block the Federal Trade Commission's proposed nonbinding, voluntary nutrition standards for marketing food to kids.

Short of marketing restrictions, city officials are trying other options. They pass laws to require menu labeling for fast food, ban trans fats, prohibit toys in fast-food kids' meals and restrict junk foods sold in schools. They propose taxes on sodas and caps on soda sizes.

Research demonstrating the value of regulatory approaches is now pouring in.

The kids living in states where schools don't sell junk food are not as overweight.

Studies of the effects of menu labeling show that not everyone pays attention, but those who do are more likely to reduce their calorie purchases. Menu labels certainly change my behavior. Do I really want a 600-calorie breakfast muffin? Not today, thanks.

New York City's 2008 ban on use of hydrogenated oils containing trans fats means that New Yorkers get less trans fat with their fast food, even in low-income neighborhoods. Whether this reduction accounts for the recent decline in the city's rates of heart disease remains to be demonstrated, but getting rid of trans fats certainly hasn't hurt.

Canadian researchers report that kids are three times more likely to choose healthier meals if those meals come with a toy and the regular ones do not. When it comes to kids' food choices, the meal with the toy is invariably the default.

A recent study in *Pediatrics* compared obesity rates in kids living in states with and without restrictions on the kinds of foods sold in schools. Guess what—the kids living in states where schools don't sell junk food are not as overweight.

Circulation has just published an American Heart Association review of "evidence-based population approaches" to improving diets. It concludes that evidence supports the value of intense media campaigns, on-site educational programs in stores, subsidies for fruits and vegetables, taxes, school gardens, worksite wellness programs and restrictions on marketing to children.

The benefits of the approaches shown in these studies may appear small, but together they offer hope that current trends can be reversed.

Researchers also suggest other approaches, not yet tried. The Yale Rudd Center has just shown that color-coded food labels ("traffic lights") encourage healthier food choices.

And Rand Corp. researchers propose initiatives like those that worked for alcoholic beverages: Limit the density of fast-food outlets, ban sales in places that are not food stores, insist that supermarkets put junk foods and sodas where they are hard to see, ban drive-through sales, restrict portion sizes and use warning labels.

These regulatory approaches are worth trying. If research continues to demonstrate their value, cities will have even more reason to use them. If the research becomes compelling enough, the federal government might need to act.

In the meantime, cities are leading the way, Richmond among them. Their initiatives are well worth trying, testing and supporting.

7

Government Intervention Will Not Solve Our Obesity Problem

Michael Marlow and Sherzod Abdukadirov

Michael Marlow is an affiliated senior scholar at the Mercatus Center at George Mason University and professor of economics and distinguished scholar at California Polytechnic State University. Sherzod Abdukadirov is a research fellow at the Mercatus Center at George Mason University.

With rising obesity and related health problems, many have called for the government regulation of the American diet. Unfortunately, past regulations have been ineffective. Worse, these "solutions" often cause other problems. The only real solution is to allow Americans to decide which diet and health products they wish to buy on the free market.

It is clear the United States is facing a rising obesity problem. But the challenge remains: We have yet to determine a successful way to tackle it. According to the National Center for Health Statistics, the prevalence of obesity among adults more than doubled from 13.4 percent in 1960 to 34.3 percent in 2008. A new report released this month by the *American Journal of Preventive Medicine* predicts that by 2030, 42 percent of Americans will be obese and 11 percent will be severely obese, or 100 pounds overweight.

Despite the myriad of studies showing American obesity is increasing, research does not clearly support that government can solve this complex problem. And yet, government solutions that provide information the public already knows— weight gain occurs when we eat too much and exercise too little—have been the focus to eliminate this epidemic.

Not only is this method not solving the problem, we may actually be increasing the social stigma associated with weight gain. Rather than pursuing a one-size-fits-all solution, we need to push back against government intervention, and allow people to find the solution that best meets their needs.

One popular government solution requires restaurant chains to post calorie counts on their menus to prevent citizens from underestimating their caloric intakes. A recent study examined the impact of New York City's 2008 law requiring restaurant chains to post calorie counts. While 28 percent of patrons said the information influenced their choices, researchers could not detect a change in calories purchased after the law. A different study in Seattle found similar evidence that their mandatory menu labeling did little to change fast food purchasing behavior.

Another government favorite, taxing sugary drinks, does more to shore up government coffers than to reduce obesity. A few studies examined the impact of increasing sugary drinks taxes by 20 percent or more. They find that higher taxes do reduce obesity, but the effect is rather limited. Interestingly, soda taxes mostly cause people without weight problems to cut back their consumption, even though they are not the intended targets of the policy. Meanwhile, frequent soda drinkers buy lower-priced soda, engage in bulk discounted purchases, and brew more sweetened ice tea.

Beyond being ineffective, there are serious harms from these state interventionist polices. Government policies are subject to intense lobbying by well-heeled interest groups, which can lead to results that are counterproductive to the problems they are trying to solve. In one case, Congress effectively declared pizza a vegetable under the intense pressure from agricultural business lobby. This allowed Congress to block attempts by the U.S. Department of Agriculture to replace pizza, which is classified as a vegetable because it contains tomato paste, with more vegetables.

Unfortunately, citizens have little choice but to pay higher taxes and obey bans when laws are passed.

Government policies may also lead to unintended consequences. Since the 1970s, Department of Agriculture dietary guidelines have urged Americans to eat low fat diets to reduce their risk of coronary heart disease and obesity. Americans heeded the government's advice to switch to foods with less fat content. But because they were eating healthier foods, they ate more. Thus, while the share of calories coming from fat decreased between 1970 and 2000, the actual amount of fat calories in their diet increased, because of an increase in overall calories.

The solutions that seem to work the best—the ones that allow individuals to tailor a plan that meets their unique needs—are given short shrift by advocates of government intervention. The growing market for diet books, health foods, weight loss centers, exercise equipment, and athletic clubs is clear evidence that people are concerned about their weight. Unlike government policies, weight loss products and ideas are tested by consumers and failures are replaced by products that really help people control their weight. Consumers will not continue to buy products that don't work.

Unfortunately, citizens have little choice but to pay higher taxes and obey bans when laws are passed. One can expect further tax hikes and bans as policymakers conclude that their well-intentioned policies failed simply because they were not harsh enough, but pushing more stringent, failed policies will not improve public health. Instead of wasting resources on inadequate solutions, consumers should return to the market for the innovative solutions, like healthy foods, gyms, and nutrition centers.

8

Government Regulation Places Excessive Emphasis on Being Overweight

Virginia Murr

Virginia Murr works for the Center for Ethics and Entrepreneurship.

In recent years, many have called for government regulation to curtail foods that are adding to the American waistline. This intense emphasis on weight loss, however, has sent a negative message to many Americans. Teens, in particular, often internalize this message—"fat is bad"—leading to anorexia and other dangerous diseases. Instead of regulating food considered unhealthy, parents should set an example for children by eating moderately.

Mayor Bloomberg of NYC [New York City] made a splash with his recent attempt to curb the consumption of large sodas, which was thwarted by the courts. Nanny State proponents, such as Bloomberg, argue that it is the government's right—and even duty—to force us, either through laws or taxation, to eat healthier in order to cut down on the rate of national obesity. Rightfully, many cogent arguments have since been made stating that food regulations and "fat" taxes violate individual rights. And, while this is the most fundamental argument against Nanny State interference with what we choose to eat or not, it isn't the only argument. . . .

Hyper Focus on Weight

There is an oft overlooked point to the debate: the message we are sending to our children when we focus so heavily on obesity. In the United States alone, up to 24 million people of all ages and genders suffer from an eating disorder (anorexia, bulimia and binge eating disorder). Let's look at these numbers a little more closely:

- A full 95% of those who have eating disorders are between the ages of 12 and 25.

- In a survey of 185 female students on a college campus, 58% felt pressure to be a certain weight, and of the 83% that dieted for weight loss, 44% were of normal weight.

- 42% of 1st-3rd grade girls want to be thinner.

- 81% of 10 year olds are afraid of being fat. . . .

It is common to hear criticism of too-skinny celebrities for being a negative influence on youth. However, the constant focus by the government, mainstream media, and even parents on obesity, I would argue, is even more guilty for influencing our children since these factors play a constant role in their lives. First, obesity is almost always presented as a horrible thing—"Too many people are obese!" "We have become a fat nation!" Then the news channels show images of morbidly obese individuals, often eating fatty foods. The message is clear: "Isn't this disgusting?"

Maybe we should be setting an example for our children by embracing moderation ourselves.

In response, people start to clamor for government intervention. Again, the message is clear: "People can't stop themselves from being fat and unhealthy, so the government must stop it." At this point, being overweight becomes not just an aesthetic condemnation, but a moral condemnation as well.

Embracing Moderation

As a woman myself and as the mother of two teenage daughters (as well as a two year old), I know the difficulty girls, in particular, experience when it comes to body image. This difficulty is compounded daily when our government-run public schools chastise children for bringing "fattening" snacks in their lunches or even take their lunches away. The message isn't missed by approval-seeking children who have yet to develop the confidence to ignore or reject overt criticism. Too many respond by embracing unhealthy dieting and eating disorders. And these decisions are merely reinforced when they hear on the news about how fat we are as a nation or they hear their parents discuss why certain foods should be banned. . . .

The fact is that it would be difficult to find a single food or drink that is inherently bad for us. It would be even more difficult to find any single food or drink that will make us overweight if ingested in moderation. So, instead of demonizing people that are overweight and the foods that may or may not play a role in making them overweight, maybe we should be setting an example for our children by embracing moderation ourselves. Maybe we should show our children what it is to accept personal responsibility for the foods and drinks we consume, for better or for worse. Maybe, just maybe, we should be teaching our children that it isn't about weight—it is about enjoying what we eat, but staying healthy enough to live long, fruitful lives.

Side Note:

Many people argue for the Nanny State against the idea of individual rights when it comes to obesity because, they claim, obese people are unhealthy and thus their medical costs are a burden to the rest of us. Assuming that this argument is valid, it still doesn't hold water. Here is why: Eating disorders are extremely hard on the human body. From vitamin deficiencies disabling the immune system to esophageal damage and even death, eating disorders create innumerable medical costs. As a matter of fact, the mortality rate associated with anorexia is 12 times higher than the death rate associated with all causes of death for females 15–24 years old. Thus, if we hold the Nanny State to its logic, they would have to start banning healthy, low fat foods right along side their banning of unhealthy, fattening foods. Before you know it, we won't have any food at all.

9

What Japan Can Teach Us About School Lunches

Dana Woldow

Dana Woldow has been an advocate for healthier school food since 2002 and shares what she has learned at PEACHSF.org.

As obesity rates for American children have grown, many have expressed concern over the unhealthiness of school lunches. In particular, much of the school lunch diet in the United States is not only non-nutritious but also fattening. This becomes especially apparent when compared with the school lunch programs in Japan and France. In both countries, the government is more heavily involved in funding and regulating school lunch programs. Americans, however, seem unwilling to embrace more government involvement with school lunches, especially if it requires more public funding.

Every so often an article pops up comparing school lunches in America to those served in other countries. To the surprise of no one, our lunches usually fare badly in comparison; this slideshow [not available] offers pictures of school lunches in America, and from around the world. How is it that so many other countries are getting school lunch right, while America continues to get it wrong?

A recent article in the Washington Post about school lunch in Japan is a must read for anyone interested in improving school food in the US. Not because the Japanese model presents a quick and easy fix to the multiple problems plaguing school food in this country, but rather because it highlights the many differences between how the subject of school food is handled in Japan, and how it is handled here.

What's for Lunch in Japan?

"Schools in Japan give children the sort of food they'd get at home, not at a stadium. The meals are often made from scratch. They're balanced but hearty, heavy on rice and vegetables, fish and soups . . . The food is grown locally and almost never frozen."

Where is lunch eaten?

"Mealtime is a scene of communal duty: In both elementary and middle schools, students don white coats and caps and serve their classmates. Children eat in their classrooms. They get identical meals, and if they leave food untouched, they are out of luck: Their schools have no vending machines."

Who eats school lunch?

"Barring dietary restrictions, children in most districts can't bring food to school, either, until they reach high school."

What is the prevailing attitude towards school lunch?

"Children are taught to eat what they are served, meaning they are prone to accept, rather than revolt against, the food on their plates. But Japan also invests heavily in cultivating this mind-set. Most schools employ nutritionists who, among other tasks, work with children who are picky or unhealthy eaters."

What is the cost, and who pays for it?

"Municipalities pay for labor costs, but parents—billed monthly—pay for the ingredients, about $3 per meal, with reduced and free options for poorer families."

Freshly prepared, locally grown food, heavy on rice, vegetables, and fish, which the children happily consume, and which cost parents only $3? How is that possible? Financially, it works because the government is covering all of the cost of labor, which is primarily cooking, since the children are serving the meal. That $3 the parents pay goes entirely for the cost of the food itself.

By contrast, the typical US school meal program spends about 45% of its budget on labor and benefits, and about 9% on overhead like delivery costs, pest control, and bank fees, leaving only about 46% for food, according to the USDA, which oversees school meals.

Japanese children are expected to eat what they are served.

So while parents in SF also pay $3 per lunch (and the state and federal government payment for a low income student's "free" lunch is $3.16), less than $1.50 of that $3 is available to pay for food. The new fresh school lunches from Revolution Foods which SFUSD began serving in January cost the district $1.95 per elementary lunch, plus about another 25 cents for milk. The fact that there is less than $1.50 in the budget to cover the $2.20 combined cost of food and milk helps drive the approximately $2 million deficit which SFUSD Student Nutrition Services incurred last year, and which threatens to go much higher this year with the new pricier fresh meals.

Because children in Japan are not generally allowed to bring lunch from home before high school, there is no stigma attached to eating school meals, because all the students eat them. Lunch is served in their classrooms, so there is no "walk of shame" to the cafeteria for low income students to get a free lunch, and everyone gets the same meal, with no "a la carte" choices for those with money to purchase them, and no vending machines to enable skipping lunch and gorging later on snacks.

With virtually all non-low income students purchasing school lunch, far more revenue flows into the Japanese school meal program than happens in most US school districts; the USDA reports that less than 50% of non-low income US students typically purchase a school lunch.

Finally, and perhaps most importantly, Japanese children are expected to eat what they are served, without complaint, but also educated to help them understand why they should be happy to eat the healthy food. This is called "Shokuiku"— "shoku" meaning food and diet, and "iku" meaning growth or education. After a 2005 report warned that Japanese children were developing poor eating habits that would lead to higher rates of obesity and diabetes, the Basic Law on Shokuiku was enacted to help all Japanese, especially children, to understand and value healthy eating habits, including a traditional Japanese diet.

In American schools, we call this "nutrition education", and it is one of the programs which suffered cuts when Congress passed the emergency extension of the farm bill on New Year's Day.

Japan isn't the only country way out in front of America when it comes to both the quality of school lunches and prioritizing the meal period as an important part of the school day. Georgeanne Brennan and Ann M. Evans have been school lunch consultants in California for over a decade. In the fall of 2011, they took a fact finding trip to France to learn about French school lunch. Their report reveals many of the reasons why school lunch in France, like school lunch in Japan, is far superior to school lunch in America.

What's for lunch in France?

Brennan and Evans describe middle school students "taking first a salad of mixed greens with slivers of chicken and several slices of chorizo, dressed with a mustard vinaigrette, and next choosing between fillet of fresh Atlantic Pollack, a type of cod, roasted with cherry tomatoes and zucchini or braised beef with mushrooms, accompanied by boiled, parsleyed potatoes and optional self-serve hollandaise sauce. Next they served themselves slices of cheese, bread, and an apple tart or piece of fruit. We watched as they settled down at their tables, each with a pitcher of water, and quietly conversed and laughed as they ate their lunch."

Who eats school lunch?

"Students can go home for lunch or eat the lunch provided by the school. Bringing your own lunch from home is not an option."

How long is the lunch period?

"The eating time is required by the Ministry of Education to be no less than 30 minutes. The elementary schools typically offer recess prior to lunch as well as after lunch, for a total of 1.5–2 hours. Schools days are typically longer, often going to 4:30."

What is the cost, and who pays for it?

"The price paid for school lunch is 2,7 Euros [about $3.60] for elementary and 3,30 [about $4.40] for middle and high school. The total cost to the school is 6,4 to 7,5 Euros [about $8.60 to $10] for elementary and 10 Euros [about $13.50] for middle and high school. The difference is funded by local, state and national subsidies."

What is the prevailing attitude towards school lunch?

"Our impression is that the French school lunch is more than a meal. It is a concerted effort by federal, regional, and local governments to teach and to model the pleasures of freshly cooked real food, the discovery of different tastes and flavors,

51

and to promote civil discourse around the table. To the French, the school lunch experience is not only a valued part of their children's educational day; it is part of learning the national culture."

What can we learn from other countries about school lunch?

As in Japan, the price non-low income parents pay for their child's school lunch is expected to cover only a small portion of the full cost of providing the meal, with the government picking up the balance. Also like Japan, French children do not bring lunch from home, although the lunch period is long enough that students can go home and have lunch with their families. With recess both before and after lunch, and a mandatory half hour for sitting at the table, French school lunch is a peaceful and enjoyable experience, unlike the "hurry up rush rush" atmosphere so common in American schools, where lunch and recess combined usually lasts less than an hour, and some schools have no recess at all. Finally, as in Japan, school lunch is viewed as an opportunity to learn about and appreciate food, and to reinforce the national culture.

American school lunch, which despite recent government-mandated improvements is still largely a pizza/hot dogs/burger/tacos experience in most schools, may be said to reinforce our national culture too, but it is a culture of fast food, of segregated lunch lines with low income children lining up for a free meal while their wealthier peers buy unregulated a la carte junk food, or rush off campus for a quickie snack from a nearby convenience store. It is a culture that pretends schools can serve up a healthy meal and pay workers a fair wage for a total cost of $3 per lunch, where government officials believe that cutting funds for nutrition education is a fair tradeoff for maintaining commodity crop subsidies for Big

Ag, and where those working towards healthier food or fewer empty calories are derided as "the food police."

What can we learn from other countries about school lunch? How about this—you get what you pay for. High quality healthy food costs more than cheap processed junk; a lunch that nourishes both body and soul cannot be created from ingredients costing a dollar and change; a respectful attitude towards eating and food is not promoted by a 15 minute lunch break; and no one benefits when school lunch policies segregate students by income. Until this country is willing to invest the kinds of resources, both financial and educational, in school meal programs that countries like Japan and France do, this is just another area where US schools will lag behind other countries.

10

Report: USDA Should Regulate In-School Snacks

Jason Koebler

Jason Koebler is a science and technology reporter for U.S. News & World Report.

The US Department of Agriculture has been more willing to regulate school lunches in recent years. Even before the results of the new programs are fully known, however, many have criticized the initiatives. Creating a healthier school lunch or school snacks works only if the children like the food. Studies, however, are lending support to the notion that a change in school lunch programs can positively impact the growing problem of obesity in children.

*A*ttempts to remove unhealthy snacks from schools could start *new controversy.*

Earlier this year, new USDA regulations on school lunches stirred up a major controversy in Washington—including a debate about whether pizza could be considered a vegetable. Now, a new report suggests the USDA should begin regulating snacks offered in school vending machines and snack lines.

The report, issued Thursday by Pew Charitable Trusts, says that high school students consume as many as 336 calories per day through snacks, and that few states offer healthy alternatives to candy, potato chips and soda. That's important considering the rise in childhood obesity over the past few decades, says Erik Olson, director of food programs at Pew. According to the USDA, reducing children's caloric intake by just 160 calories per day can have a huge impact on obesity.

"That's the difference between eating an apple or eating a bag of chips a day," Olson says. "It doesn't take huge changes in their diet."

But any attempts to further regulate in-school food options is likely to have plenty of critics. Steve King, a Republican Congressman from Iowa, says it'd be "another overreach of the nanny state."

"I think Michelle Obama wants to be the Dietician-in-Chief. It's a gross overreach of the federal government to step in and ration food to kids," he adds. "None of these students get overweight on school lunches. The source of the problem is junk food at home and a lack of activity," he adds.

The Healthy, Hunger-Free Kids Act of 2010 required the USDA to update its school lunch guidelines and also contained provisions requiring the agency to update its guidelines for food sold outside of school lunch programs. The USDA updated its lunch guidelines earlier this year, but hasn't yet updated snack guidelines. According to a USDA spokesperson, the agency has "asked for additional time to review the proposed standards for competitive foods to ensure that we do what is right for kids in a way that is workable to the school districts that will be charged with implementation."

In a June statement, U.S. Secretary of Agriculture Tom Vilsack said that a snack rule would have to be "something that is doable, something that's workable, something that we can defend, and something that won't be successfully attacked."

In September, King and fellow Republican Congressman from Kansas, Tim Huelskamp, introduced the "No Hungry Kids Act," which would repeal the USDA rules regarding school lunch standards and prohibit upper caloric limits on school lunches. King says that students in his state have turned to snacks as a way to stave off hunger during the school day.

"If we don't get enough to eat, we grab something sweet till the next time we're getting a real meal," King says. "Students are grabbing for sweets in order to supplement that diet. The solution is to give students more of the healthy, nutritious food they need."

A fresh fruit or vegetable is great unless it ends up in the trash.

Olson takes issue with critics' assertions that schools aren't providing students enough food.

"Prior to the new guidelines, high schools were offering an average of 857 calories, the new limit is 850 calories," Olson says. "The big difference is that the calories are from healthier foods. We're not trying to get rid of snacks in schools, we're suggesting that they be healthier."

Huelskamp says he supports giving children healthier food, but in schools he's visited, students simply don't like some of the new options.

"You can't force kids to eat with a one size-fits-all approach. A fresh fruit or vegetable is great unless it ends up in the trash can," he says. "The USDA mandate didn't work on lunches and it wouldn't work on a snack mandate."

In August, the journal *Pediatrics* released a study that found states with stricter school snack laws had lower childhood obesity rates. According to the study, "laws that regulate competitive nutrition content may reduce adolescent BMI change if they are comprehensive, contain strong language, and are enacted across grade levels."

In an April letter to Vilsack, groups such as the American Academy of Pediatrics, Pew, Kraft Foods, and Nestle asked that the agency consider "authoritative scientific recommendations for nutrition standards" when devising its snack food guidelines.

The Pew study found that in every state but New Hampshire, less than 50 percent of high schools offered fruits as snacks, while many high schools sell salty or sweet snacks. The study, based on data from the 2011 Centers for Disease Control School Health Profiles report, only measured which foods were offered, not which ones students were consuming.

"The study is flawed," Huelskamp says. "How can you make a claim about what the impact [of a snack mandate] might be if you can't measure down to an individual level?" The Pew report recommends that the USDA limit calories on individual snack foods, set limits on sugar and fats, and place restrictions on high-calorie beverages.

King takes issue with that last part: "They've put every kid in America on a diet. Now it looks like Michael Bloomberg's no large sodas in New York ordinance could be applied at the federal level," he says.

11

Regulating School Lunch Oversteps Government's Authority

Brian Vanyo

Brian Vanyo is the author of The American Ideology: Taking Back Our Country with the Philosophy of Our Founding Fathers.

Recently, students have begun protesting changes in school lunch programs. At the root of the problem is new policy enacted by the federal government. The federal government began influencing the school lunch program during the 1930s, clearly overstepping its constitutional boundaries. Because the federal government has no constitutional role in school lunches, students should continue to protest these policies.

Students around the nation are protesting reduced-calorie lunch menus mandated by new, restrictive federal regulations. First championed by First Lady Michelle Obama, these regulations were designed to improve lunch nutrition standards but instead have left students starving for more food. Students everywhere have begun speaking out against the new mandates on websites and blogs. One Kansas high school even created a video parody titled "We are Hungry" . . . to object to the new regulations—the students' recommendation: "Set the policy on fire!"

These protests certainly draw attention to this draconian bureaucratic policy. But they also ought to serve as a wakeup call to every American that our federal government has been slowly stealing our liberty and growing its power over time.

Usurping the School Lunch Program

Just look at how the federal government has taken control of school lunch menus. To begin with, the Constitution, which establishes the federal government's limited authority, says nothing about a federal power to regulate school lunch menus—this power is actually reserved to the States under the Tenth Amendment. In fact, for almost 150 years under the Constitution, the federal government had nothing to do with school lunches. (And I'm aware of no student malnutrition epidemic in America during this time.) And then came FDR [Franklin Delano Roosevelt].

Our Founding Fathers recognized that the path toward tyranny is often paved by progressive assaults on individual liberty.

In the 1930s, President Franklin Delano Roosevelt instituted a number of radical economic policies (labeled "fascist" by Italian Fascist leader Benito Mussolini) that transformed the federal government into a domineering national force—into what FDR described as an "economic autocracy." FDR played on the people's shaken confidence in free markets during the Great Depression to consolidate power in the executive branch, which had become so powerful by 1936 that he acknowledged it could "provide shackles for the liberties of the people." Among the economic powers assumed by FDR was a power to set quotas on farm production to prop up food prices. The federal government also purchased farm surpluses to maintain higher prices, and it began distributing these surpluses as direct welfare and to support school lunch programs. (Prior to this, the Supreme Court struck down similar federal redistributive programs, but it soon changed its tune during FDR's reign.) The federal government has involved itself in school lunch programs ever since, expanding its influence along the way.

The federal government soon enlarged the school lunch program with the National School Lunch Act of 1946. The program grew again with the Child Nutrition Act of 1966. Amendments to this act in 1968 provided more funding for meals during summer programs. Amendments in 2004 promoted healthy food choices, but specified that they be designed and implemented at the local level. And most recently, the Healthy Hunger-Free Kids Act of 2010 authorized the federal government to set nutrition standards throughout the country, including ridiculous calorie limits that have outraged hungry students all across the nation.

It is clear that the Constitution grants the federal government no authority to regulate school lunches.

The Limits of Federal Authority

Long ago, our Founding Fathers recognized that the path toward tyranny is often paved by progressive assaults on individual liberty. (I wrote about this in my new book, *The American Ideology: Taking Back our Country with the Philosophy of our Founding Fathers.*) For example, James Madison once observed that, throughout world history, "there have been more instances of the abridgment of the freedom of the people by the gradual and silent encroachments of those in power than by violent and sudden usurpations." He therefore advised the American people to watch out for the government's minute advancements against their liberty—encroachments that may be tolerable alone, but become intolerable when compounded in time. Madison wrote:

The people of the United States owe their independence and their liberty to the wisdom of descrying in the minute tax of 3 pence on tea, the magnitude of the evil comprised in the precedent. Let them exert the same wisdom in watching against every evil lurking under plausible disguises and growing up from small beginnings.

The federal government's regulatory control over school lunch menus clearly grew up from small beginnings and has gradually expanded in time. And many Americans have become ever more conditioned to the government's exercise of this illegitimate authority, given the force of its precedent. As Thomas Paine once wrote, "[A] long habit of not thinking a thing *wrong*, gives it a superficial appearance of being *right*, and raises at first a formidable outcry in defense of custom."

We must not fall into this trap. It is clear that the Constitution grants the federal government no authority to regulate school lunches (and so many other facets of the American economy). So we should not stand for a policy that claims the power to do so. What we need is a president who will uphold the Constitution and act on the hungry pleas of students everywhere in America. We need a president who will "set the policy on fire!" And if the fire happens to consume the other 34,000 pages of federal regulations, then so be it.

12

Government Regulation of Sweeteners Should Be Considered

Tom Laskawy

Tom Laskawy is a founder and executive director of the Food & Environment Reporting Network and a contributing writer at Grist.

While many commentators have reacted negatively to the Nature *article calling for the regulation of sugar, they should be listening more closely to scientists. Excessive sugar in the American diet is creating a number of health-related problems. While many regulatory methods have been tried, there is a need for a concerted, national effort. At the very least, however, the* Nature *article has led to a vigorous debate of the issue.*

A recent op-ed published in the journal *Nature*, by several scientists who are experts in their field, has the pundits all aflutter. But the subject is somewhat surprising: Sweeteners. . . .

Robert Lustig (a minor YouTube celebrity since his 2009 lecture on fructose), Laura Schmidt, and Claire Brindis argue that added sweeteners of all kinds—including sugar, high-fructose corn syrup, and all their oddly named ilk (that means you, maltodextrin!)—have as many negative health effects as alcohol and should be regulated.

Responses have come from all over the food politics spectrum—from Raj Patel in *The Atlantic*, who took to dreaming of a world where large corporations aren't in charge of feeding us, to Jennifer LaRue Huget on the *Washington Post's* Checkup blog, who just wants everyone to leave such issues to personal responsibility.

Others have expressed scorn toward the group of scientists for addressing policy at all. This opinion can be summed up by a tweet from reporter Dan Mitchell that read, "Scientists need to set a much higher bar for proposing policy measures."

Listening to Scientists

Now, I agree that policy expertise is its own animal. But when it comes to science-related policy—climate change, genetically engineered foods, water quality, and toxic substances, to name a few—I think policymakers could stand to pay a wee bit more attention to what scientists have to say.

Our biggest health problem isn't obesity. It's metabolic disorders like diabetes, hypertension, high cholesterol, cardiovascular disease and non-alcoholic fatty liver disease.

Even so, my sense is that the true importance of this op-ed is getting lost in all the knee-jerk "to nanny or not to nanny" responses. You see, in their abstract, the scientists wrote, "Added sweeteners pose dangers to health that justify controlling them like alcohol." This no doubt takes the reader to an immediate and very particular place. I mean, are we talking about only serving sugar in bars? Needing a "sugar license"? Has the world gone mad?!

The grammarian in me says that shifting the clauses around to read, "Like alcohol, added sweeteners pose dangers to health that justify controlling them," makes for a meaning that's closer to what I think the authors were going for, and puts the focus on the general similarities rather than implying that we should, say, pass a constitutional amendment prohibiting sugar.

The Dangers of Sugar

Let's focus on the authors' core assertions:

1. Our biggest health problem isn't obesity. It's metabolic disorders like diabetes, hypertension, high cholesterol, cardiovascular disease and non-alcoholic fatty liver disease. And sweeteners play an outsized role in the worldwide epidemic of these conditions. As the authors put it:

> ... 20% of obese people have normal metabolism and will have a normal lifespan. Conversely, up to 40% of normal-weight people develop the diseases that constitute the metabolic syndrome. . . . Obesity is not the cause; rather, it is a marker for metabolic dysfunction, which is even more prevalent.

In short: Fat but Fit FTW [For the Win]!

2. Added sweeteners meet the four criteria for government regulation set out in social psychologist Thomas Babor's 2003 book *Alcohol: No Ordinary Commodity*, which are "now largely accepted by the public-health community." Those criteria are: "unavoidability (or pervasiveness throughout society), toxicity, potential for abuse and negative impact on society."

3. Governments in the U.S. and abroad have been slow to acknowledge the above and remain focused on saturated fat and salt, which, it turns out, contribute less to metabolic disorders than we used to think.

4. Several of today's popular solutions aren't really working. Research has shown that "school-based interventions that teach children about diet and exercise" don't demonstrate any meaningful benefit. Taxes, meanwhile, don't do enough on their own to lower consumption.

As I see it, these are the points we should be discussing. Not whether we need to add sugar to the name of the Bureau of Alcohol, Tobacco, and Firearms. In fact, taxes, marketing restrictions, and limitations on availability are all *already* being tried. (On that last one, the article references a group of parents in Philadelphia who have attempted a tough form of age restriction—they physically block the entrance to corner stores when schools let out to prevent kids from buying sugary drinks or snacks.)

A National Effort

Efforts like these *are* common, but they're still haphazard—and they're mostly taking place at the local level. That fact simply makes it easier for food companies to control the debate—as it appears they've been able to do with junk food vending machines in elementary schools.

Indeed, every one of the authors' suggestions is being attempted in some form somewhere in the United States, just not effectively or broadly enough to make a difference.

What Lustig and his collaborators really want us to understand, I think, is that the science behind sweeteners' metabolic effects requires a more rigorous, national effort. And that rather than focusing on soda alone, for instance, we should include all products with added sweeteners. Sadly, it doesn't seem like that's the takeaway for most readers.

Still, this op-ed did accomplish one thing—it has gotten lots of people debating the potential dangers of sugar and the need for regulation. And that's a good place to start.

13

Sugar, Cheese and Other Dietary Demons

Jennifer LaRue Huget

Jennifer LaRue Huget is a freelance writer and an author.

Excessive sugar and fat in the American diet have prompted a call for regulation. Unfortunately, many regulations fail to work because most people dislike being told what to eat. Recent studies have singled out sugar and cheese, arguing for wider regulation to protect Americans from themselves. If moderation is to prevail, however, the government will need to take a more positive approach to food regulation.

When I was a young adult working in one of my first professional, go-to-the-office jobs, I often brought lunch to eat at my extremely not-private desk. An older, portly woman named Gertrude, on more than one occasion, tsk-tsked me for my food choices. Admittedly, I didn't always bring ultra-healthful foods for lunch. But her criticism made me want to dig in with even greater gusto—and then visit the vending machine, just for good measure.

The point is that nobody likes a nag, and scolding people—or punishing them, or making them feel guilty—for their food choices is as likely as not to backfire. People don't like being told what to eat or what they shouldn't eat.

Sugar, Cheese and Other Dietary Demons

Sugar Consumption

I've been thinking about Gertrude today in light of two recent public-health developments. First, just in time to cast a pall on Valentine's Day, health experts from the University of California, San Francisco are calling for government regulation of sugar. In a commentary ... published Wednesday afternoon [February 2012] in the journal *Nature*, Robert Lustig and colleagues argue that sugar poses as great a risk to public health as alcohol and tobacco and that therefore its use should be restricted.

The commentary spells out how excessive consumption of added sugars—defined as "any sweetener containing the molecule fructose that is added to food in processing"—can harm the human body; from contributing to high blood pressure and triglycerides to causing liver damage, the possibilities extend beyond simply making people fat.

The authors make the case that sugar consumption in the U.S. is excessive and has increased as our access to and liking for packaged, processed foods have risen. They don't spell out precisely how much sugar is too much; nor do the current Dietary Guidelines for Americans set a limit on how much added sugar (as opposed to the natural sugar inherent in fruits, for instance) we can have.

I think any effort to restrict access to sugar should be approached with care.

The authors note that cutting back on Americans' sugar intake will likely require making it harder, and more expensive, to purchase sugar-containing foods. They of course suggest some kind of tax, and they even go so far as to propose an age restriction for buying sugar-sweetened beverages, with kids under, say, 17, barred from buying sodas. Ending government subsidies of sugary foods could help, too, they write.

(They do note, though, that soda tax programs haven't taken hold or proven useful in lowering people's soda intake.)

A Moderate Approach

Even as the sugar debate continues, the folks at the vegan-diet-promoting Physicians Committee for Responsible Medicine [PCRM] have attracted attention for their graphic billboards portraying cheese as the food responsible for making us fat. PCRM founder and president Neal Barnard has been quoted as saying that the ideal amount of cheese in our diets would be no cheese at all.

In my humble opinion, the world would be a sad place without cheese. And though I'm no longer a big fan of sweets, I think any effort to restrict access to sugar should be approached with care. Reading the report in *Nature* practically made me want to pour a bag of plain sugar into my open mouth, in sheer defiance of anyone's telling me what I can and cannot eat.

This is why I like the federal government's newish MyPlate program, which is based on the advice in the 2010 Dietary Guidelines for Americans. That document and MyPlate take a positive approach to nutrition advice; they encourage us to eat fruits, vegetables, lean protein and whole grains without telling us to skip sugar, salt and fat altogether. Instead, they gently suggest we cut back on those ingredients. In other words, MyPlate's not a nag.

Yes, far too many of us are overweight or obese, and many of us may suffer ill health effects from eating too much sugar and/or too much cheese. There's got to be a way to help people moderate their diets in such a way that they can enjoy foods of all kinds without going overboard.

But my advice to anyone coming up with ideas for what other people should and shouldn't put in their mouths: Remember Gertrude. If you come off sounding like her, people will surely rebel.

14

Government Regulation Is Needed to Reduce Sodium in the American Diet

National Academy of Sciences

The National Academy of Sciences is a private, nonprofit institution that provides expert advice on some of the most pressing challenges facing the nation and the world.

A report by the Institute of Medicine has called for the regulation of salt in the American diet. Even as the federal government has attempted to educate Americans on the dangers of sodium, sodium levels have increased. Since educational methods have failed, it is time for the US Food and Drug Administration to regulate sodium levels. While new regulations would take time to put in place, voluntary efforts by restaurants and the food service industry could help speed up the transition.

Washington—Reducing Americans' excessive sodium consumption requires establishing new federal standards for the amount of salt that food manufacturers, restaurants, and food service companies can add to their products, says a new report by the Institute of Medicine. Because the vast majority of people's sodium intake comes from salt that companies put in prepared meals and processed foods, this regulatory strategy would make it easier for consumers to eat lower, healthier amounts of salt, said the committee that wrote the report.

The U.S. Food and Drug Administration [FDA] should gradually step down the maximum amount of salt that can be added to foods, beverages, and meals through a series of incremental reductions. The goal is not to ban salt, but rather to bring the amount of sodium in the average American's diet below levels associated with the risk of hypertension, heart disease, and stroke, and to do so in a gradual way that will ensure that food remains flavorful to the consumer, the committee said.

Failed Education, Increased Sodium Intake

Regulatory action is necessary because four decades of public education campaigns about the dangers of excess salt and voluntary sodium cutting efforts by the food industry have generally failed to make a dent in Americans' intakes, the committee said. The industry's voluntary efforts have fallen short because of lack of a level playing field for all products. Companies have feared losing customers who could switch to competing products or brands with higher salt content. Also, salt is so widespread and present in such large amounts in grocery store and menu items—including many foods and drinks that people do not think of as salty—that it is difficult for people who want to reduce their sodium intake to succeed.

"For 40 years we have known about the relationship between sodium and the development of hypertension and other life threatening diseases, but we have had virtually no success in cutting back the salt in our diets," said committee chair Jane E. Henney, professor of medicine, University of Cincinnati College of Medicine, Cincinnati. "This report outlines strategies that will enable all of us to effectively lower our sodium consumption to healthy levels. The best way to accomplish this is to provide companies the level playing field they need so they are able to work across the board to reduce salt in the food supply. Lowering sodium by the food industry in a stepwise, monitored fashion will minimize changes in flavor and still provide adequate amounts of this essential nutrient that are compatible with good health."

On average, Americans consume more than 3,400 milligrams of sodium—the amount in about 1.5 teaspoons of salt—each day. The recommended maximum daily intake of sodium—the amount above which health problems appear—is 2,300 milligrams per day for adults, about 1 teaspoon of salt. The recommended adequate intake of sodium is 1,500 milligrams per day, and people over 50 need even less.

Americans' salt consumption has been shaped in part by changes in eating habits as people consume more processed foods, dine out more frequently, and prepare fewer meals from basic, raw ingredients in the home. U.S. residents have gradually grown accustomed to saltier foods as the amount of salt in the nation's food supply has increased over time, but research indicates that this trend can be reversed as well. People's tastes can be reset to prefer less salty flavor through subtle reductions overtime, studies show.

Implementing Changes

FDA has the authority to regulate salt as a food additive, the report says. As a substance that has been added to foods throughout history, salt has been treated as "generally recognized as safe," and there are no regulatory limits on its use as an additive. But studies connecting high intakes of sodium to high blood pressure, heart attacks, strokes, kidney disease, and other debilitating and deadly conditions show that salt is safe only up to a certain amount. FDA will need to gather and assess an ample body of data to determine what limits to set on the mineral's use in processed foods and prepared meals and what the incremental decreases should be. The committee acknowledged that establishing the process will take significant time, staffing, and funding.

The percentage of Daily Value for sodium on food packaging—which tells shoppers how much of their recommended daily intake is in a serving of the product—is based on an earlier maximum level of 2,400 milligrams per day. Because using an upper level can lead people to mistakenly think that it is a desirable amount, the committee recommended that the Daily Value for sodium be changed to reflect the adequate intake for adults of 1,500 milligrams per day.

Given that it will take time to develop and implement FDA's new regulatory process for salt, restaurants, food service firms, and food and beverage manufacturers should pursue voluntary sodium reduction efforts in the meantime, the committee said. These initiatives could provide experiences and information that could help FDA shape the standards and incremental decreases.

15

Government Should Not Regulate the Sodium Content of Food

Joel C. Brothers

Joel C. Brothers writes about food topics at the Professor's House.

Most governments have the bad habit of trying to control all aspects of citizens' lives. Unfortunately, new regulations have a cost in personal freedom. Sometimes, as in the case of sodium, the perceived problem does not even exist. Salt is necessary for the human body. Furthermore, many of the supposed negative aspects of salt—such as hypertension—have not been proven. The government has no business regulating sodium in the American diet.

Wherever you live, one thing is common to most countries. The governments are always trying to control everything . . . just because they think they can. There is always some sort of crisis that the government must 'save' you from, whether or not there is any evidence that it is actually a problem. For Nazi Germany, it was Bolsheviks and Jews. In China and other places it is dissidents. In the Middle East, it is U.S. Imperialism. In the US, it switches from drugs, private ownership of firearms, religious fanatics, militias, etc. . . . The latest 'crisis' is from evil food producers that force us to eat too much salt, and very large food portions, all against our will. And every crisis that is managed means we lose a little more personal freedom. But the government has to do it, because, after all, we are much too stupid to be able to read the labels on our food, and make our own decisions. And our government does such a good job administering things like illegal drug use, drivers licenses, and even the federal budget ... it begs the question: Should government regulate the amount of salt in our food?

There has not been a single recorded death exclusively and directly attributable to salt consumption.

First, it may be a good idea to find out if this is really a problem in the first place. Political organizations such as the FDA [US Food and Drug Administration] tell us that eating too much salt causes hypertension and heart attacks. Is this true? There have been many studies done on this very subject, but for some reason, this research is largely ignored. We can start with a few basic facts that are indisputable:

- Salt is made up of two essential minerals that your body absolutely has to have to function at all; Sodium, which is vital for nerve functions, muscle contractions, water retention, and other essential biological processes, and chloride, which the body has to have to regulate metabolism and PH balance. Without these two minerals, you will most certainly die.

- Since 1924, in the United States, iodine, an essential mineral the body needs for regulating hormones, has been added to 'Table' salt (as opposed to 'canning', and 'pickling' salts), virtually eliminating iodine deficiencies in most of the developed world. If you cut out salt, you'll be cutting out a significant source of iodine as well.

- Without salt, life in very hot and humid regions would be difficult, because salt helps your body hold on to water longer, and staves off dehydration.

- Salt is not stored in the body, and excess amounts are eliminated through normal metabolic processes.

- Salt is a vital ingredient in many foods that prevents bacterial growth and controls moisture content.

- Salt is an all-natural additive that is present in most things in nature. It is not a chemical, or synthesized additive, unlike the absolutely harmful MSG [monosodium glutamate], which governments seem unwilling to regulate.

Now for the Cons

Fib: Salt causes high blood pressure and heart attacks.

The Truth: The only way they came up with this is '*Biological Plausibility*', meaning it just sounds good, but has no evidence to support it. In fact, a 1972 study indicated that a reduction in salt could actually have some negative biological effects. . . .

To date, there has not been a single recorded death exclusively and directly attributable to salt consumption. Salt can temporarily aggravate an existing case of hypertension due to more water in the blood, but it does not cause the condition. High Blood Pressure is caused by other factors, such as age, general health, obesity, lifestyle, stress, and genetic propensity.

Fib: Americans consume 2+ times the safe amount of salt.

The Truth: There has never been a "safe" or "dangerous" level of salt consumption established through normal scientific means. As long as fresh drinking water is available, excess salt is eliminated. Salt Toxicity has only been observed in confined animals fed with ridiculously high levels of salt, and denied access to drinking water. This results in dehydration. We consume a lot of salt because we consume a lot of food, more than any other nation on Earth. We are the most obese group of people on the planet. This is due to two main factors: Prosperity and technology. We are the world leaders in both areas. We eat more because we can.

Fib: Reducing the amount of salt in processed foods will save millions of lives.

The Truth: Reducing salt will cause people to eat more, or not buy reduced salt products. It would also have a negative effect on some foods such as cheese and breads, that depend on salt for texture, sanitation, and leavening. There are already reduced-sodium products available, and they only make up a very small portion of sales.

All of the available and reliable data indicate that regulating salt in foods is an attempt to usurp more power by seemingly addressing a problem that does not exist. Can government regulation affect our health and safety? Of course. They could make a law that says you have to be in your house by 9:00 PM every night to curb crime, and that you will be imprisoned if you are more than 20 pounds over-weight, and you can only drink water, and eat organic salt and sugar-free foods. Sure, you may live longer, but is this a really desirable situation? I think not. You can control your salt intake yourself, easily, by simply reading labels and asking questions. What we really need is less government, not more. Think about that the next time you ask yourself, "*Should government regulate the amount of salt in our food?*"

16

Will Fast Food Turn Healthy Next Year?

Matthew Yglesias

Matthew Yglesias is the business and economics correspondent for Slate *magazine.*

One unnoticed element in recent federal healthcare legislation would require chain restaurants to offer more extensive labels. While this would not guarantee that Americans would eat healthier, the labeling would allow individuals to make healthier choices if they wished. The real change, however, will come from more health-conscious restaurants that offer fast food. Americans, then, will continue to eat fast food, labels or not. The question is whether there will be healthier fast food choices.

One of the least-noticed elements of Obamacare [the Patient Protection and Affordable Care Act] is a federal rule requiring chain restaurants to post calorie counts on their menus starting in 2013. Similar laws have been enacted already on a state or local basis in several jurisdictions, but it's only now that the policy is going national that it really makes sense for companies to start building strategic decisions around it.

That corporate decision-making is the key to whether the new rule drives meaningful gains in public health. If chains continue to emphasize maximum fat at minimum cost, eating habits probably won't change much. But if the labeling regulations really emphasize the dangers of high-fat foods and the benefits of fruits and vegetables, it could encourage healthier eating.

Labeling's Impact on Chain Restaurants

One chain that seems potentially poised to benefit is Chop't Creative Salad Company, a D.C. and New York chain that's a personal lunchtime favorite of mine and sells what some would consider outrageously expensive salads. When I asked founder Tony Shure about the new law last week, he wasn't incredibly eager to engage, noting that "very few people find politics appetizing," an allusion to the significant backlash against restaurateurs who've been whining about higher labor costs as a result of the Affordable Care Act. But he did say that "the days of secret sauce are over," and clearly health-conscious consumers are an important part of their market.

Still, salads are a very small part of the chain restaurant industry. Sweetgreen, a rival salad company, has 15 locations in the D.C. and Philadelphia areas and offers slightly smaller salads. Mix't Greens, with a somewhat higher price point, withdrew from the East Coast but seems to be doing all right in California. Even Freshii—the most aggressively expansionist of the salad chains—has just more than 30 U.S. locations.

A big difference between home cooking and dining out is the opacity of the production process.

But the giants that dominate the chain restaurant market are adjusting to menu labeling, too. McDonalds, smartly, de-cided to get ahead of the curve by launching menu labeling even before the election so the company could start the learn-ing process before the competition. They're also touting a "Fa-vorites Under 400" list of low-calorie options. Tellingly, packaged-food giant Unilever promoted a Seductive Nutrition

Challenge over the summer to encourage restaurateurs to try to reformulate existing menu favorites into lower-calorie versions.

These upstream impacts on business thinking are important because most studies of consumer behavior show that the menu information per se causes only small changes in consumer decision-making in either adults or children.

Historically, a big difference between home cooking and dining out is the opacity of the production process. That means a major competitive advantage in the food game is finding ways to pack more cheap, unhealthful fats into foods than people would be comfortable deliberately serving themselves. Whole menus and franchises have been built around this, and just putting the numbers on the wall doesn't change that. But chain restaurants are the factories of our time, and with new rules they'll have reason to turn their R&D [research and development] departments to the task of developing healthier options. And if the McDonaldses and Pizza Huts of the world can't find a way to adapt, they're potentially vulnerable to disruption by the handful of chains who've already hit the ground running with concepts that are more health-friendly.

This relatively undebated element of the new health care law could end up being one of the most significant.

Healthy Fast Food

There's no guarantee, but if positive change does come to people's eating habits, that will be the mechanism. Efforts like Slow Food USA or *Mother Jones* food writer Tom Philpot's dictum that "from-scratch cooking is absolutely the most powerful tool we have for improving our diets and resisting the food industry's most awful offerings" are patently unrealistic.

Many people, myself included, enjoy cooking as a hobby. And it's common for mass production to coexist indefinitely alongside artisanal methods or hobbies. Neither knitting nor custom-built furniture has vanished from the landscape, but home production of these items isn't economically significant. Living standards improve because mass producers get better at making things, not because people turn backward to inefficient small-scale methods. Eating is no different. If the worst of fast food is replaced by anything, it will be better fast food. Companies are out there trying to make it happen, and so far they're succeeding in niche markets. Policies forcing more and more obvious disclosure of nutritional information should help the process along by at least creating a situation where firms that succeed in designing more healthful options have a way to credibly turn that into a business advantage.

It very well might not work. But diet and nutrition are arguably more important drivers of health than health care per se, and almost all of us eat more often than we see the doctor. So if a changing regulatory environment does encourage shifts in business models, this relatively undebated element of the new health care law could end up being one of the most significant.

17

Pizza Shop Owners, Grocers Decry Pending Obamacare-Linked FDA Labeling Rules

Neil W. McCabe

Neil W. McCabe is a senior reporter at Human Events.

A labeling provision in federal healthcare legislation will create a big problem for fast food franchises. Part of the problem is the sheer number of choices and combinations; for example, the number of topping options consumers have when ordering a pizza. The increased labeling also will cut into fast food franchise and grocery store profits. Currently, there are efforts being made to amend the healthcare legislation, using common sense to achieve more workable results.

*A*nother unhappy surprise for businesses hidden in the 2000-page *Patient Protection and Affordable Care Act.*

Operators of restaurant and supermarkets are fighting new FDA rules for implementing section 4205 of President Barack Obama's Patient Protection and Affordable Care Act that will force the labeling of fresh made food as packaged food.

"It's just ridiculous that they would make us spend so much money for so little useless information to go to the consumer," said Jonathan D. Sharp, who with Jackie, his wife of 25 years, owns and operates two Domino's stores in Abilene, Texas.

The former Air Force cryptologic Russian linguist said nothing in his code-breaking background helps him understand the rule. "We need to send it through one of the computers at NSA to decrypt it."

As the rule, which the FDA calls: "Nutrition Labeling of Standard Menu Items at Chain Restaurants" is still being written, people affected do not know what they will be doing right or wrong, said Sharp, who after the Air Force joined Dominos and worked his way up until he was a supervisor of nine retail locations in the Philadelphia-area. As a supervisor, he had the opportunity to buy the two stores he has now.

"We don't know what the penalties are, what the enforcement rules are going to be—there is very little we know about doing this wrong," he said. "All we know about doing it right is that it is going to cost a lot of money."

The rule is a burden, but Sharp would not close his doors, he said.

---

95 percent of food items sold in groceries stores are already covered by existing packaging and labeling regulations.

"It will eat into profitability, of course," he said. "For different franchisees, it will mean different things, for some it would come out of their pockets, for others it would putting off maintenance or not spending as much on marketing—there are all sorts of ways we can absorb the $5,000, but it's the opportunity cost that keeps us from spending it on another thing."

Just more upsetting to Sharp is the fact that more than 90 percent of the Domino's business is delivered, less than 10 percent of the customers will ever see the posters.

Erik R. Lieberman, a regulations attorney with the Arlington, Va.-based Food Marketing Institute, said although grocery stores and supermarkets were not part of the PPACA, the FDA expanded its mandate to include those retailers into the rules for section 4205.

Lieberman said 95 percent of food items sold in groceries stores are already covered by existing packaging and labeling regulations.

The five percent of food items not covered come from the bakeries, deli counters and products, such as soups, sandwiches and salad bars, he said.

"The store supplies its own ingredients for the items that are prepared inside the store," he said. "If we have a lot of carrots, we may improvise and make carrot soup or put more carrots in the chicken soup, so things are always changing."

It will cost the supermarkets and grocery stores $1 billion to implement their compliance programs.

"This law was designed for standard items at fast food restaurants, it was modeled after the New York City law, which was aimed at restaurants like McDonalds," he said.

Lieberman said the White House Office of Management and Budget has already estimated that the paperwork burden on supermarkets and grocery stores require 15 million man-hours to comply with the new FDA labeling rules.

It will cost the supermarkets and grocery stores $1 billion to implement their compliance programs with hundreds of millions of dollars in costs to maintain compliance, he said.

Another example of the rules overreach, the FDA asserted jurisdiction over chains with 20 or more outlets, and a chain is any collection of retail operators who share identity, he said. This interpretation means that the thousands of members of

the Independent Grocer Association, now known simply as
IGA, are part of a chain, even though it is an alliance of independent stores.

Mellissa Cummings, a brand ambassador with the Ann Ar-
bor, Mich.-based Domino's corporation, which opened its
10,000 store in September, said the FDA is applying the same
accuracy within 20 percent standard that it applies to packaged foods.

"We are trying to get food out the door," she said.

---

*There are 34 million possible combinations to the pizzas
and other items sold at a Dominos.*

There is a huge effort to train employees and to standard-
ize portions, she said. "You could have that is heavy-handed
on one order and go light on the next—that is just the reality
of the restaurant world and the fresh, handmade products."

Sharp said one of the frustrating things to the Dominos
franchisee is that for more than 12 years, Dominos customers
have been able to go online to not only order and track a
pizza, but also design their pizza to order with the company's
"Cal-o-meter" a function that produces a precise accounting
of the nutritional make up of the pie as they designed.

Given the possibilities, there are 34 million possible combinations to the pizzas and other items sold at a Dominos, he
said.

Cummings said grocers and the members of the pizza industry are confident Congress can set the FDA straight with
"The Common Sense Nutrition Disclosure Act of 2012." The
bill is sponsored in the House by Rep. John R. Carter (R.-
Texas) and Sen. Roy D. Blunt (R.-Mo.).

The legislation would dial back the 20 percent standard to
a "reasonable basis" for determining the ingredients and nutri-
ents with consideration for inadvertent human error, she said.

A restaurant for the purposes of the rule would have to derive at least 50 of its revenues from fresh and handmade food, she said.

When he announced that he had filed the bill July 24, Carter said his bill was meant to end the chaos.

"The Affordable Care Act was a 2,000-page bill, and most House members had no idea it created new federal regulations on pizza toppings and sub sandwiches," he said.

"But the threat of fining a business because a teenage employee put two extra slices of pepperoni on a pizza goes from crazy to scary."

Organizations to Contact

The editors have compiled the following list of organizations concerned with the issues debated in this book. The descriptions are derived from materials provided by the organizations. All have publications or information available for interested readers. The list was compiled on the date of publication of the present volume; names, addresses, phone and fax numbers, and e-mail and Internet addresses may change. Be aware that many organizations take several weeks or longer to respond to inquiries, so allow as much time as possible.

American Academy of Pediatrics (AAP)
141 Northwest Point Blvd., Elk Grove Village, IL 60007-1098
(847) 434-4000 • fax: (847) 434-8000
website: www.aap.org

The American Academy of Pediatrics (AAP) is an organization of pediatricians committed to the optimal physical, mental, and social health and well-being for all infants, children, adolescents, and young adults. The AAP offers continuing medical education programs for pediatricians and issues policy statements, clinical reports, clinical practice guidelines, and technical reports. *AAP News* is the official newsmagazine of the AAP, and *Pediatrics* is its official journal.

American Dietetic Association (ADA)
216 West Jackson Blvd., Chicago, IL 60606-6995
(800) 877-1600
website: www.eatright.org

The American Dietetic Association (ADA) is the world's largest organization of food and nutrition professionals. ADA seeks to improve the nation's health and to advance the profession of dietetics through research, education, and advocacy. Articles, research findings and the *Journal of the American Dietetic Association* can be accessed online.

American Heart Association

National Center, 7272 Greenville Ave., Dallas, TX   75231
(800) 242-8721
website: www.americanheart.org

The American Heart Association is a national voluntary health agency that promotes cardiovascular health. The website provides important information on how to recognize signs of heart attack, stroke, and cardiac arrest. Information also can be found about a wider range of diseases and conditions and about smart choices to benefit a healthy lifestyle.

American Psychological Association (APA)

750 First St. NE, Washington, DC   20002-4242
(202) 336-5500 • fax: (202) 336-5708
e-mail: public.affairs@apa.org
website: www.apa.org

The American Psychological Association (APA) aims to "advance psychology as a science, as a profession, and as a means of promoting human welfare." It produces numerous publications, including the monthly journal *American Psychologist*, the monthly newspaper *APA Monitor*, and the quarterly *Journal of Abnormal Psychology*.

Center for Science in the Public Interest (CSPI)

1875 Connecticut Ave. NW, Suite 300, Washington, DC   20009
(202) 332-9110
website: www.cspinet.org

The Center for Science in the Public Interest (CSPI) considers itself to be the organized voice of the American public on nutrition, food safety, health, and other issues. CSPI seeks to educate the public, advocate for government policies that are consistent with scientific evidence on health and environmental issues, and counter industry's powerful influence on public opinion and public policies. CSPI supports food labeling campaigns and government efforts aimed at reducing the amount of sugar, salt, and fat Americans eat.

Centers for Disease Control and Prevention (CDC)
Division of Nutrition and Physical Activity (DNPA)
1600 Clifton Rd., Atlanta, GA 30333
(800) 232-4636
e-mail: cdcinfo@cdc.gov
website: www.cdc.gov/nccdphp/dnpa/

The CDC is part of the National Institutes of Health (NIH), Department of Health and Human Services (DHHS). Its Division of Nutrition and Physical Activity (DNPA) has three focus areas: nutrition, physical activity, and overweight and obesity. The DNPA addresses the role of nutrition and physical activity in improving the public's health. DNPA activities include health promotion, research, training, and education. The DNPA maintains an overweight and obesity web page, on which it provides research-based information for consumers.

Coalition for Responsible Nutrition Information
(866) 764-0701
e-mail: info@nationalnutritionstandards.com
website: www.nationalnutritionstandards.com

The Coalition for Responsible Nutrition Information seeks to provide consumers with comprehensive nutrition information about the food they consume while dining out so they are able to make healthy and informed decisions about their nutrition. The organization's website offers information about legislation regarding food labeling and recent news articles on the topic.

Eunice Kennedy Shriver National Institute of Child
Health and Human Development (NICHD)
31 Center Dr., Building 31, Room 2A32, MSC 2425
Bethesda, MD 20892-2425
(800) 370-2943 • fax: (866) 760-5947
e-mail: NICHDInformationResourceCenter@mail.nih.gov
website: www.nichd.nih.gov

The Eunice Kennedy Shriver National Institute of Child Health and Human Development (NICHD) is one of the twenty-seven institutes and centers that comprise the National Institutes of Health. The NICHD conducts and supports research on topics related to the health of children, adults, families, and populations. The NICHD has established a wide reaching initiative to generate long-term solutions to childhood obesity. The NICHD website provides child health statistics, backgrounders, and many other resources.

Food Research and Action Center (FRAC)

1875 Connecticut Ave. NW, Suite 540, Washington, DC   20009
(202) 986-2200
website: www.frac.org/index.html

The Food Research and Action Center (FRAC) is the leading national nonprofit organization working to improve public policies and public-private partnerships to eradicate hunger and undernutrition in the United States. FRAC has published several papers about the link between hunger and obesity, and works with hundreds of national, state, and local nonprofit organizations, public agencies, and corporations to address this and other food-related problems plaguing Americans.

National Institute of Diabetes and Digestive and Kidney Diseases

31 Center Dr., Building 31, Room 9A06, MSC 2560
Bethesda, MD   20892
(301) 496-3583
website: www.niddk.nih.gov

The National Institute of Diabetes and Digestive and Kidney Diseases conducts and supports research on serious diseases. The website provides information about research opportunities and the diseases that affect public health.

Rudd Center for Food Policy & Obesity

Yale University, New Haven, CT   06520-8369
website: www.yaleruddcenter.org

The Rudd Center for Food Policy & Obesity is a nonprofit research and public policy organization devoted to improving the world's diet, preventing obesity, and reducing weight stigma. The Center serves as a leading research institution and clearinghouse for resources that add to the understanding of the complex forces affecting how we eat, how we stigmatize overweight and obese people, and how we can change.

Bibliography

Books

Wenonah Hauter   *Foodopoly: The Battle Over the Future of Food and Farming in America*. New York: New Press, 2012.

Kirk Kardashian   *Milk Money: Cash, Cows, and the Death of the American Dairy Farm*. Durham, NH: University of New Hampshire Press, 2012.

Frederick Kaufman   *Bet the Farm: How Food Stopped Being Food*. Hoboken, NJ: Wiley, 2012.

John Lusk   *The Food Police: A Well-Fed Manifesto About the Politics of Your Plate*. New York: Crown Forum, 2013.

Michael Moss   *Salt Sugar Fat: How the Food Giants Hooked Us*. New York: Random House, 2013.

Marion Nestle   *Eat Drink Vote: An Illustrated Guide to Food Politics*. New York: Rodale, 2012.

Marion Nestle   *Food Politics: How the Food Industry Influences Nutrition and Health*. Los Angeles: University of California Press, 2013.

Marion Nestle and Malden Nesheim   *Why Calories Count: From Science to Politics*. Los Angeles: University of California Press, 2012.

Robert Paalberg   *Food Politics: What Everyone Needs to Know.* New York: Oxford University, 2010.

Michele Payn-Knoper   *No More Food Fights! Growing a Productive Farm and Food Conversation.* Indianapolis, IN: Dog Ear, 2013.

Michael Pollan   *Cooked: A Natural History of Transformation.* New York: Penguin, 2013.

Peter Pringle   *Food Inc.: Mendel to Monsanto.* New York: Simon & Schuster, 2010.

Marie-Monique Robin   *The World According to Monsanto.* New York: New Press, 2012.

Melanie Warner   *Pandora's Lunchbox: How Processed Food Took Over the American Meal.* New York: Scribner, 2013.

Parke Wilde   *Food Policy in the United States: An Introduction.* New York: Routledge, 2013.

Periodicals and Internet Sources

Arkansas Business   "Menus to Start Counting Calories," March 11, 2013.

Lindsey Coblentz   "Shaking Up the Soda Industry," *Food Manufacturing,* November–December 2012.

Richard Corbett "Soft Drinks—Industry Can Avoid Rising Tide of Regulations," just-drinks.com, May 24, 2013. www.just-drinks.com.

Vanessa Drucker "Fizzy Drinks and the US Economy," FundWeb, November 5, 2012. www.fundweb.co.uk.

Economist "The Nanny State's Biggest Test: Government Intervention," December 15, 2012.

Entertainment Close-up "Academy of Nutrition and Dietetics Praises USDA's Changes to Standards for All Foods Sold in School," July 7, 2013.

Krystal Gabert "Safety First: Disasters, Mishaps, and Recalls," *Food Manufacturing*, June 2013.

Julie Gunlock "Big Brother at Your Table," *National Review*, May 20, 2013.

Dean Heyl "IFA Fighting Discriminatory Chain and Fast-Food Restaurant Ordinances and Laws," *Franchising World*, June 2013.

Jack Kenny "Profit from Regulations: The Continuing Expansion of Nutritional Labeling Means Business for Converters," Label & Narrow Web, March 13, 2013. www.labelandnarrowweb.com.

Adam Leyland	"'Our Industry Is Suffering from Health Regulation Fatigue,'" *Grocer*, March 30, 2013.
Maclean's	"A Surprisingly Refreshing Aftertaste," March 25, 2013.
Modern Healthcare	"Regulatory Morass: Lawmakers Work to Clarify Policies for Compounders," November 19, 2012.
Money Life	"Sweet Idols—Part 1: Are You Eating More Sugar than Required?" July 1, 2013.
Money Life	"Sugar Idols—Part 2: How Celebrities Promote Harmful Sugary Drinks," July 2, 2013.
Self	"Sure Looks Like Feel-Good Food," August 2012.
Jacob Sullum	"The Peril of Palatability: A Former FDA Chief Sounds the Alarm About Dangerously Delicious Food," *Reason*, November 2009.
Michael Tennant	"Globesity: How Globalists Are Feeding Off the Obesity Crisis," *New American*, February 4, 2013.
Connie Tipton	"Shed the Programs that Impede Innovations and Growth," *Dairy Foods*, November 2012.

Index

A

Abdukadirov, Sherzod, 39–42

Advertising messages, 13–14, 36

Alcohol: No Ordinary Commodity (Babor), 64

American Academy of Pediatrics, 56

American Heart Association, 37

American Journal of Preventive Medicine, 39

American Progress (magazine), 8–9

American Psychological Association, 14

B

Babor, Thomas, 64

Ban of soda size. *See* Soda size ban

Barnard, Neal, 68

Basic Law on Shokuiku, 50

Bittman, Mark, 28

Bloomberg, Michael, 7–10, 22–25, 31–34

    See also Soda size ban

Blunt, Roy D., 84

Bowden, Jonny, 26–30

Brennan, Georgeanne, 50

Brindis, Claire, 13–14, 62

Brothers, Joel C., 73–76

Bureau of Alcohol, Tobacco, and Firearms, 64–65

C

Cardiovascular disease, 64

Carolla, Adam, 27

Centers for Disease Control and Prevention (CDC), 7–8

Centers for Disease Control School Health Profiles report, 57

Chain restaurants, 78–79

Child Nutrition Act (1966), 60

Childhood obesity, 8, 54, 56

Cigarette bans, 12–15, 36

Circulation (magazine), 37

CKE Restaurants, 24

Corn Refiners Association, 28

Cummings, Mellissa, 84

D

Daily Value for sodium, 71–72

Dasani water, 29

Dehydration, 75

Diabetes, 8, 19, 28, 50, 64

Dietary guidelines, 41, 67, 68

Dietary Guidelines for Americans, 67

Dyslipidemia, 18

E

Eating disorders, 44–46

Evans, Ann M., 50

F

Farley, Thomas, 32

Fast food

    in chain restaurants, 78–79